MOVING UP
THE ORGANIZATION
IN FACILITIES
MANAGEMENT

Proven Strategies to Increase
Productivity in Your Workforce

A. S. Migs Damiani
CPE/F•AFE

SciTech Publishing, Inc.
Mendham, NJ

*This book is dedicated
to all facilities professionals
who are interested in furthering
the professional status of facilities management
in their respective organizations.*

Printed in the United States of America

10 9 8 7 6 5 4 3 2 1

ISBN 1-891121-04-9

Scitech books may be purchased at quantity discounts for educational, business, or sales promotional use. For information, contact the publisher:

Scitech Publishing, Inc.
89 Dean Road
Mendham, NJ 07945
www.scitechpub.com

CONTENTS

ABOUT THE AUTHOR

A.S. MIGS DAMIANI, *CPE/F•AFE*

 A. S. Migs Damiani is President of The Donohoe Companies' Mechanical Systems Operations Division, commercially known as Complete Building Services (CBS), which maintains more than 13 million square feet of space in the Washington metropolitan area. CBS is a leading provider of facilities operation and maintenance services including design review, facility inspections/audits, energy conservation programs, computerized maintenance management system (CMMS) programs, indoor air quality (IAQ), installation, repairs and maintenance, and operation and management of many different types of facilities.

Prior to joining CBS in 1994, Migs was the Director of the Department of Facilities and Services for Montgomery County, Maryland. His department provided real estate, design and construction, maintenance and a myriad of services to all agencies (excluding schools) of the Montgomery County Government, involving more than 190 buildings. Migs was formerly President of COM•SITE International, a firm specializing in data center planning, construction and maintenance; Director of Corporate Facilities/Administrative Services for Planning Research Corporation and Manager, Corporate Facilities for Fairchild Industries. He has spent more than 30 years as a corporate facilities executive, serving as president or reporting directly to board chairs and company presidents. As a representative of the owner, he has been responsible for the design, development and maintenance for more than 125 major building projects.

Migs holds a B.S. degree in Commerce and Engineering from Drexel University and a Masters in Engineering Administration from The George Washington University. He has been named Plant Engineer of the Year by The American Institute of Plant Engineers (AIPE), recently renamed The Association for Facilities Engineering (AFE), and is a Fellow of AIPE and an Honorary Life Member of the American Institute of Architects (AIA). Migs is the author of *Looking for the Gold*, a values-based book that focuses on total quality in facilities management; *Creative Leadership: Mining the Gold in Your Workforce*; more than 60 technical articles; six cover features; and chapters in two hi-tech real-estate books.

Migs is a graduate of The Center for Creative Leadership and has been a guest lecturer at The George Mason University, Georgetown University, The University of Maryland, Penn State University and James Madison University. He has received more than 30 national awards in his distinguished career and is a frequent speaker at national engineering and maintenance conferences. Migs also conducts specialized "people skills" training for industry, government agencies, colleges and universities, hospitals and professional societies.

PREFACE

I developed this book as a companion document to my recently published book, *Creative Leadership: Mining the Gold in Your Workforce* and encourage you to obtain a copy. In mid-1994 I wrote my first book *Looking for the Gold: A TQM Success Story,* expressly for facilities professionals and you may obtain a copy of that book by calling 1-800-488-8040.

Corporations and government want/demand more leaders in facilities management and the above books provide you with useful information toward that end. Both peer and top management review has been excellent and I am confident that you will benefit from it.

Please feel free to write, call or e-mail me with your comments or questions.

A.S. Migs Damiani, CPE/F•AFE
President
Complete Building Services
2101 Wisconsin Avenue, NW
Washington, DC 20007
(202) 333-4977
(202) 342-5199 FAX
E-mail: migsd@donohoe.com

1

THE ENGINEER AS MANAGER

Companies need more leaders in their organizations, people who are not only technically competent in their field but can also energize and motivate others in order to increase productivity and be more competitive globally. People are the heart of productivity and unfortunately are often the most ignored in a company. And yet, the only thing a company has that the competition does not have is their employees. This is often the difference maker. A leader's main job is to grow employees and when he or she does that, it is amazing what people will do and how productive they will become.

Facilities management is generally more ignored by top management than others in that it is considered overhead, inefficient and nonproductive. Many organizations consider the function to be middle management at best and often, it reports to other managers of administrative services, personnel, finance or plant operations. Seldom will the head of facilities be a vice president or even report to a president, vice president or chief financial officer of a corporation. In the 1990s the function has become ripe for outsourcing. Many companies have outsourced, downsized and pushed down the facilities management function even further in the organization.

The good news is that a facilities professional can move successfully up the organization by attaining leadership and financial skills. Technical people do have followers; i.e., others who have

1

similar skills and hope to learn more through mentoring. Learning leadership skills will allow the facilities professional to maximize the effectiveness of subordinates through organizing groups of technical people, staffing in a way that matches jobs with talents; delegating and empowering intelligently; communicating more and more effectively; managing time better; and moving successfully from engineer to manager (and leader).

To move up in the organization, change must occur in people's attitudes, behavior and interpersonal skills. That is what this book is all about. *Moving Up the Organization in Facilities Management* specifically addresses what our profession should do and in a "how-to-do-it" fashion. It should be read in conjunction with *Creative Leadership: Mining the Gold in Your Workforce* and *Looking for the Gold,* two other books I have written. These books supplement what you will learn and were written with your needs in mind.

Simply put, to be successful in *facilities management, you must have:*

- a positive attitude
- people skills
- business sense
- technical competence

Success in facilities management depends on one's ability to educate and inform top management and others of your many contributions, especially those related to the bottom line; to be the best you can be technically; and to develop/reinforce your business skills and people skills. You should renew your commitment to the profession, focus on your weaknesses and hone your leadership skills–sharing your vision and energizing and inspiring your employees to be the best they can be. To accomplish the latter, you must have, and maintain, a positive attitude and develop a positive, caring work environment.

Today, and in the future, you must prove your value and worth to the company in order to make a difference, adding enough value so everyone can see that something very important would be missing if you left. To do this, you first must stand back and identify weaknesses and then focus on them while developing a sound, strategic plan.

Listed below are the thirteen common challenges/problems of facilities management that keep us back in the pack with the others. Meeting these challenges and solving these problems will go a long way toward your success. Doing so will require constant attention and continual emphasis; however it will be worth the effort you put into it.

THIRTEEN COMMON PROBLEMS
MADE IN FACILITIES MANAGEMENT

1. Do not communicate enough with top management, our employees, and other departments.
2. Do not work hard enough to overturn the poor image of maintenance.
3. Do not make good presentations or sell ourselves and our ideas well.
4. Do not understand how to use financial information to our advantage.
5. Are not as computer proficient as we should be; i.e., we are not aware of, or do not use, the decision support (management applications) provided by the computer as well as we could.
6. Resist change, especially when management has financial/emotional ties to existing equipment or systems.
7. Are not productive.
8. Do not measure the effectiveness of our performance.
9. Do not focus enough on the process.
10. Do not mentor enough.
11. Do not train enough, especially in the areas of people skills and leadership.
12. Do not have high expectations of ourselves.
13. Do not take the lead.

Examine these problems as if you were looking at your organization from top side or as a customer. I do hope you agree that they are *real* problems that need to be addressed and solved. Only after accepting the fact that we have weaknesses and then identifying them, can we strengthen them. Look especially at maintenance, since that function, by its very nature, is inefficient and unproductive. Based on my experience, that is the area that's been most troublesome to progress made in our profession and the most difficult to manage and lead. Therefore I have concentrated on this particular problem and offer solutions in the following sections and pages that should be helpful to you in changing the image of maintenance.

Facilities management is challenging and an important part of a company's success. Its leaders determine what role it plays and where it stands or will stand in the organization chart. It can and will rise to the top if you want it to. The material in this book will assist you in reaching your goals and objectives. Good luck.

2

LEADERSHIP

Achieving Greater Success
in Facilities Management

Facility managers can do a great deal to improve the way they are regarded by top management. A recent advertisement for a senior managerial position in facilities management demonstrates what is important for us to succeed in our profession. It called for the following abilities and experience:

APTITUDE
- degree in engineering or architecture
- professional registration, advanced degrees in engineering, architecture or business; certification in the profession is highly desirable
- significant senior management experience with large, complex facility operations
- financial management of large, complex budgets

ATTITUDE (PEOPLE SKILLS)
- supervising and motivating senior professionals and managers
- nurturing a productive, empowered work force
- strong oral and written communication skills

5

- management style that emphasizes openness
- intradepartmental and interdepartmental cooperation and support are expected
- skill in dealing with many diverse constituents is required

Pursue these carefully. How can you become more proficient in those attitudinal qualities (people skills) listed?

Our profession has changed a great deal during the 1990s and we can reasonably expect it to stay the course in the near future. Change is here to stay. Companies will continue to downsize and outsource, and demand even more productivity and creativity from their leaders. We must literally do the work of those who "went away" due to downsizing and this takes away from our time available to "coach," "lead" and "communicate" with our employees. However, the Internet is, and will be, a wonderful tool for us, allowing us to obtain information in a fraction of time it once took us and leaving us with more time to coach, lead and communicate with our employees.

A positive attitude, good interpersonal skills, business sense and technical competence are the skills we'll need to acquire to stay ahead of the curve and prevent "executive obsolescence," and prepare ourselves for promotion.

We can also expect growing competition for fewer middle management positions that exist today and will exist in the future. The ideal facilities manager should have a technical background but if he/she is not well versed in financial and interpersonal skills, and can't effectively work with others and motivate staff; someone with those skills will be selected for the top facilities positions. An active membership in professional societies such as Association for Facilities Engineering (AFE), Association of Physical Plant Administrators (APPA), International Facilities Management Association (IFMA), Property Management Association (PMA), American Society for Healthcare Engineering (ASHE), and others will provide you with the opportunity to acquire many of the skills you will need to meet these demands.

Facilities management and especially maintenance, is seldom viewed by top management as a bottom-line contributor. In fact, if top management could do without the maintenance operation they would get rid of it in a heartbeat and they have done that in the 1990s. As a matter of fact, many companies have outsourced the operating and maintenance (O&M) functions of their business. I believe that has occurred because we are not communicating the value of what we do to our senior management and/or peers. If we were, outsourcing facilities would not be occurring as often as it is.

Educate your boss and the rest of your management team, making them aware of the many positive contributions maintenance is making to the bottom line. The definition of good maintenance is to protect and preserve. It isn't easy to justify maintenance as a "value added" service because its image is poor and many owners have not been educated in the value of maintenance. Investing in a good maintenance program will pay dividends by preserving assets and saving money, especially in utilities cost, and extending the life of the asset. Communicate often and with personal resolve, and you'll find many doors of opportunity will open before your eyes.

Given a choice, top management will appoint or promote individuals with a business sense and people skills over those who are better qualified technically. Acquire these skills and you'll be unstoppable. Begin today by focusing on your and your employees' training needs and fulfilling them. You can attend seminars/workshops on leadership and network with accomplished facilities professionals who have risen to those positions you are seeking. Become certified as a CPE, CFM, CPM, RPA, FMA and/or CFEP. Ask someone you respect in the profession to mentor you. Perhaps you can even get your management to send you to the Center for Creative Leadership's Leadership Development Program. You won't know if you don't ask.

Top positions in our profession should be filled by technically competent people but they won't, if we don't acquire leadership skills as well. You can do it! As corporate scrutiny of the bottomline intensifies, those who head facilities must exhibit good technical abilities and even better management skills.

Let's look closer at the four skills needed to become a winner in our profession–a positive attitude, good interpersonal skills, good business sense and technical competence. These important skills are covered throughout the book.

3

THE MEASURE OF SUCCESS IN FACILITIES MANAGEMENT

You surely have noticed that major corporations are "contracting out" much of their maintenance and support work. The trend is most visible in mailrooms, messenger services, security services, custodial services, copy centers, computer operations and maintenance functions and it is likely to continue to be a standard in the industry.

In a 1990 article in *The Wall Street Journal*, Peter Drucker said that in-house service and support activities in many organizations have become de facto monopolies with little or no incentive to improve productivity. He also said that management of in-house support services is not likely to do "the hard innovative and often costly work that is required to make the service work productive." Because of this attitude, he added, "when in-house support departments are criticized for doing a poor job, the reaction is to hire more staff, thereby increasing costs with little chance of improving productivity or efficiency."

"Systematic innovation in service work is as desperately needed as it was with machinery in the 50 years between Frederick Winslow Taylor in the 1870s and Henry Ford in the 1920s," said Drucker. "Each task, each job has been analyzed and then reconfigured. Practically every tool has to be redesigned." The answer, he concluded, is to unbundle clerical, maintenance and support work to independent outside contractors. "Productivity increases in support work will only happen when it is done by separate, freestanding enterprises."

Forty years ago service and support costs accounted for no more than 10 to 15 percent of total costs. Today, they are likely to take 40 cents of every dollar and can no longer be brushed aside. Facilities management is a business whose emphasis must be in line with the corporation's emphasis. In these times, corporate emphasis is on financial strength and liquidity with the objectives of improving cash flow, cost containment, cost reduction, cost avoidance and increased productivity. That same emphasis should be shared by facilities management.

During these times, the impact on the facilities management function is two-fold:

- Management has greater expectations. Facilities management will be expected to do more for less and to do it more quickly.
- There will be greater opportunities. Facilities management now has a receptive audience for projects that impact productivity, costs, quality, customer service and profitability.

We should recognize that facilities management is a financially-based job, and facility managers should continually demonstrate to management that they are a financial asset in terms that management can understand and appreciate, such as cost savings.

Let's focus on how the "in-house" facilities management function can forge and carry out the vision of managing facilities as a vital corporate asset rather than being a target to trim, downsize or outsource. Unfortunately, the latter is occurring all too frequently. This can be prevented and facilities managers can obtain positive attention and proper recognition by top management of their significant contributions to the success of the company.

MISCONCEPTIONS ABOUT FACILITIES MANAGEMENT

Historically, top management has paid little attention to their facilities' functions. It was generally felt that facilities management does not contribute to the bottom line, and the association with maintenance and services, which has the poor image of being inefficient and costly, has been a hindrance to most facilities management departments. This attitude seems to have been heavily influenced by two misconceptions, which may be called the *percentage approach* and the *efficiency approach*.

The percentage approach arises from the point of view that maintenance expenditures constitute only a small percentage of sales and the image of most maintenance departments is poor. Progress in maintenance has been poor; basic elements of management (planning, organizing, staffing, directing, and controlling) are lacking in many facilities organizations; and associated with maintenance are high costs, personnel starting late and quitting early, waiting, walking, idle time, poor materials handling, inadequate supervision and quality control. Two-person maintenance (when one could do the job) and unions have also prevented progress made in maintenance.

Although unions have been a good source of training for maintenance personnel, their seniority system and trades specialization philosophy and inflexibility has hindered the progress of maintenance. Here are a few examples:

In order to install a bathroom fixture, unions would require the following craftspersons—a rigger, plumber, laborer and sometimes an electrician, to be employed when only a plumber might be needed to do the job. Seniority systems and other "pay-related" issues also affect productivity and cost of maintenance. All craftspersons receive equal pay, which is an inhibitor to performance and an expensive way to do business. Should a more productive employee get the same pay as someone much less efficient? Of course they shouldn't, but they do, and it dampens the enthusiasm and eventually the productivity of the better workers. Seniority also affects productivity and morale in many organizations. During downsizing the person who has been there the longest often stays instead of a younger, more productive and less expensive employee.

The inflexibility of unions sometimes affects a company's ability to be competitive. For example, in today's world we need every competitive advantage that we can get. In maintenance, cross training and use of multi-skilled craftspersons are a necessity in order to become efficient and effective but they are seldom found in union shops.

The efficiency illusion is reflected in observing that maintenance departments appear only to be efficient when they keep production moving by the successful handling of emergencies and infrequent, major projects. By observing only the unusual and infrequent, management fails to recognize the large number of routine maintenance jobs that are being handled in an efficient manner.

THE MEASURE OF SUCCESS

Successful facilities managers are not only achievers but also leaders. They have a knack for getting things done, know the business of the business and inform those above them in terms of achievement related to the corporation's goals. To succeed, today's facilities managers must:

- Possess considerable political, organizational leadership and communication skills
- Know the business well
- Be part of the top management team
- Possess a strong engineering or technical background
- Be able to understand and manage technology and experts in the field

- Be a planner
- Be a manager of managers
- Educate top management
- Be able to demonstrate how effective facilities management contributes to a competitive edge of this company
- Be able to measure the effectiveness of facilities management and its contribution to the corporation

As corporate scrutiny of the bottom line intensifies, those who head facilities must exhibit good technical capabilities and even better management skills. The ideal facilities manager should have a bachelor's degree in engineering and an MBA. Given a choice, in most cases the applicant with the MBA will be selected by top management to head the facilities organization.

It is important that the facilities manager be a leader and always think as a leader, not just as a manager. Recognize that leaders are needed at every level of business and society. It is important also to keep a positive outlook, which is difficult to do, because part of the facilities manager's job is to say "no" at times and to listen to complaints. It is also important to have good interpersonal and communication skills and, also, to learn to listen well. The person who is speaking should always know that you are listening, and more importantly, that you understand what they are saying.

And it is important to develop a good business sense and to understand the financial structure of your company. Understand the balance sheet, the profit and loss (P&L) statement and budget, and learn to communicate your positive efforts with numbers. The facilities manager must have knowledge of the company's vision or direction and be a willing and active participant in the strategic planning process. This will have a positive impact on management.

If your facilities management operation is not getting the recognition you feel it deserves, you have three options available to you. You can:

- Move up
- Move over
- Move out

There are always a lot of obstacles to moving up that must be overcome. The list below, while not exhaustive, illustrates these obstacles:

- Company size
- Organizations with no vision
- Management that is ignorant (uninformed)
- Reductions in middle management (downsizing, rightsizing)
- Outsourcing options
- Mergers
- Economy
- Organizational structure
- Organizational politics
- Staffing workforce
- Lack of cash
- Lack of capital

The successful facilities manager has to deal with these types of roadblocks in most organizations. Many of the obstacles above can be overcome and viewed as opportunities by those who have the will to succeed.

A PROFESSION OF CHANGE

During the twenty-first century, facilities management will truly be a changing industry. Many corporate-based services will be outsourced to achieve better management, economy and efficiency. Facilities organizations alone are not being singled out. Such reorganizations have been occurring for some time in information services, accounting and generally throughout the corporate structure. Don't be surprised to see entire facilities organizations outsourced with facility managers leaving and contracted back, working in the same position but for another company.

Rapid advancements in technology will force change and the current business climate, and newer trends in management thinking; i.e., downsizing/rightsizing and eliminating middle management will cause changes that are much different from anything we've ever experienced. Leasing, short-term solutions and cash flow/liquidity solutions will naturally cause outsourcing to be a dominant factor in the years ahead. Those who understand their corporation's strategic objectives and who align their departmental goals with those objectives will fare well in the end.

FOURTEEN WAYS TO GAIN
TOP MANAGEMENT'S ATTENTION

Facilities management seldom receives top management's attention, unless of course something goes wrong. And who wants that kind of recognition? Positive attention and proper recognition can best be achieved by demonstrating bottom-line contributions, and success will come to those who effectively communicate the impact to his/her superiors through demonstrated proficiency.

Success can be achieved in a number of ways. The following suggestions will go a long way in helping you get the attention of top management:

1. Know the business of your business. This is easier said than done, however, it is essential. Your department's contributions should be measured against the company's goals and objectives and other strategic planning initiatives. Facilities departments should be prepared to endure both progress and back sliding when either is in the company's best interests. As indicated earlier, there is an increasing emphasis on management rather than technical competence, and the facilities manager must keep up with the state-of-the-art technology and be flexible enough to turn on a dime with programs that are in keeping with the company's strategic plans.

2. Improve the image and efficiency of maintenance and other support services. Take a hard look at the department and stop accepting mediocrity. Maintenance is generally viewed as the most nonproductive department in a plant, with minimal standards and quality, ineffective labor, scheduling and some maintenance techniques dating back 100 years. Part of a manager's job is to study outsourcing as an alternative to onboard facilities management. Take an objective look into all aspects of maintenance to see if positive results can be obtained through outsourcing. Perhaps outsourcing is a better answer. If you aren't concerned and proactive in this area, someone else in top management will do the job for you.

3. Educate your boss. As stated earlier, management is usually ignorant (meaning uninformed) regarding the positive contributions made by facilities managers. We all believe that the boss knows a lot about what we do. He doesn't and can't, unless we tell him, and it is not only proper but also essential that we do communicate. Remember, communication should be in terms that top management can understand and shouldn't be done in a self-serving manner. It is important for top management to know the positive side of facilities management, especially as it affects the bottom line.

4. Document your savings, cost containment, costs avoidance, productivity increases. Every time you make or save money, report it. Compile reports on a weekly, monthly, quarterly and yearly basis and ensure that they get into the right hands. You'll be surprised at year end of your accomplishments.

5. Think bottom line. In most cases every dollar saved in overhead is a dollar added to the bottom line. Some managers spend every penny they receive in approved budgets because they feel that they will receive less the following year. This is a sure way to fail. Zero-based budgeting, by line item, should be a standard practice with a hard comparative look taken at the costs of outsourcing alternatives, which in some cases can be less expensive and more efficient than in-house solutions.

16

6. Look for opportunities to make money. You can be an out-sourcing alternative to someone else. There are many documented cases where one company is performing services for another or two companies have combined resources to keep O/M costs at a minimum. Try something new and creative, get rid of what you don't do well, and get better at what you do well.

7. Write articles and speak to groups. Share your expertise and experience. Most companies are highly supportive of outside involvement of employees and publicize these activities in their company newsletters. That's one way of communicating to, and gaining the attention of, top management. Also, the experience you gain in writing and speaking is valuable training; one which will help you sell ideas inside your organization. And you will always learn from the audience.

8. Participate in professional societies/community organizations. Most companies are good corporate citizens in that they give back to the community they serve. Companies take pride in those employees who serve their community. Become active in professional societies, company-sponsored functions, community service and in the political process and you will be recognized in a positive manner. Teaching in-house seminars as well as outside the company in your area of expertise also will be widely recognized. You will be provided opportunities for leadership positions and be honored for your accomplishments.

9. Take the initiative and speak up. Be proactive and make your views known early in a positive, constructive manner. Accept and positively respond to criticism rather than being negative and defensive about it. Learn to say "no" tactfully to requesters of service who make impossible or unrealistic demands and better yet, look for ways to say "yes" and work cooperatively with others. And don't be a complainer–solve the problem, don't be a part of it.

17

10. Motivate others. Learn to lead and be a leader, a manager of others. Lead by example–work early, stay late, make decisions expeditiously, give credit to others, and answer phone calls promptly. These are examples of good work habits which others should follow. Let people know that you respect others who get the job done, no matter how busy they are.

11. Plan, plan, plan. Plan your department's work and your work to be in step with your company's plans. Plan ahead and *follow up*. Proper planning is the key to accomplishment.

12. Understand financials. Those who can fully understand financial statements seem to progress much faster in their careers. It is important to express your plans in a manner that presents financial impacts of various alternatives and can evaluate the alternatives in an objective manner. Financial expertise is of growing strategic importance in today's increasingly challenging and competitive environment.

13. Train, train, train. Keep others trained as well as yourself. The importance of training can't be overemphasized, especially training that is tied into organizational goals. Specific training that focuses on converting weaknesses to strengths is generally most helpful and yields the most results from training moneys available. Remember, few people quit while in training.

14. Be a "changemaster." View change as an opportunity that will yield better results. Most people resist change and must be educated as to the value of the change that is occurring. Today, and in the future, change will be a way of our working life and rapid adjustment and adaptability to change is essential. Leaders lead change.

A new level of facilities manager has emerged over the last decade, one who has come out of the backroom and takes on responsibilities other than pure facilities under their wings. Today's successful facilities manager is administratively trained and is adaptable to any condition that affects his/her company. They are leaders who are capable of managing all services and show no fear of change. In fact, they relish change and the opportunities that change brings.

Today's facilities managers are able to communicate effectively on all levels. They are strong and well respected by their peers, as well as top management. They listen and give credit where credit is due. They are planners and organizers who "follow up" well and care for their company, their profession and their fellow employees, in that order.

The above is a prototype description of today's facilities manager. If you desire to advance in the profession, these characteristics should be helpful. Coupled with these suggestions, you should–over time–be able to bolster the image of your department and gain the recognition you deserve from top management.

Success can be defined in one word: *achievement.* Organizations are built around people, and the successful person is the one who gets things done, without complaining. To achieve success, most of us encounter failure along the way, and we must learn to deal with failure by not dwelling on losses, but by setting our sights on what lies ahead. Failure is an important part of the success process.

Finally, it is essential that you plan specific goals with a deadline for their achievement. Important ingredients of this planning should include:

- A burning desire to accomplish goals
- A supreme confidence in yourself and your abilities–never think of defeat, always have a "can do" attitude, concentrate on your strengths rather than your weaknesses
- Following up – be determined and consistently follow through on your plan regardless of obstacles, criticism or what people think, say or do
- Understanding corporate culture–place emphasis on client, company, employees and lastly, self and continuously work toward developing and maintaining a positive, caring environment

4

SUCCESSFUL DESIGN
AND CONSTRUCTION
MANAGEMENT

Managing the planning, design and construction of facilities and project management are areas in which facilities managers can get a lot of positive attention from top management because both areas have high visibility in corporations. I have been fortunate in my career to be named the owner's representative for more than 125 major building projects, including two large corporate headquarters complexes. As the head of large facilities organizations, I have also administered many projects that were considered critical by my management. The following two chapters look at these areas in a manner that will help you do a better job and gain more recognition in your company.

Construction today is a team effort. Planners, engineers, suppliers, manufacturers, building contractors, and construction managers must all work together and understand each other's function. However, the key to the success or failure of any building project is the owner or his/her agent. As representative for the owner, the facilities manager is the leader of the team and the ultimate decision maker.

As buildings become more sophisticated, owners or plant engineers must increasingly rely on the independent architect/engineer (A/E) for design, and on the contractor for construction. The facilities manager's responsibility is now a matter of finding the right experts for the job, and communicating the project requirements to that expert.

Troublesome areas that affect contract performance arise in the technical and administrative stages of a construction project. Here are some practical suggestions that have proved useful in resolving the most frequent sources of contention.

Owner Preparation. When beginning a project, the owner should plan his/her needs and formulate a detailed program of requirements (scope of services) for the consultant's reference. Performance by the A/E is directly dependent on the owner's understanding of the project requirements. As is frequently noted in work involving computers, good input generates good output. At this stage:

- Be as detailed as possible in writing the program of requirements. The construction cost estimate and the time allotted for design are based on this program.
- Allow sufficient time for design. The facility when built will probably last a lot longer than anyone on the original design team.
- Be prepared to pay reasonable fees that allow the performance of a top-quality job, including the construction support aspect.
- Determine construction costs based on the program, with the consultant's help. Generally, that estimate becomes part of the contract as a budget objective (fixed limit of construction).
- Try to reduce the program in size and not in quality, if the estimate is higher than the budget. Function and life-cycle considerations such as energy conservation and maintainability should receive top priority. Aesthetics are a secondary issue, subject to economics. Communicate this principle to the consultant at the outset.

Consultant Selection. Selection of a suitable A/E is important to the owner because he/she must rely heavily on the A/E's professional judgment.

It may be useful to keep in mind that the consultant's task is difficult and complex. Consultants must be familiar with and conform to all codes, which in many cases are subject to interpretation; they must provide good-quality drawings and specifications, and be knowledgeable of construction practices. In addition to servicing the individual client, consultants must possess marketing know-how, they must have some knowledge of the laws affecting their work, they must be familiar with cost estimating, and also function as bill collectors.

The following guidelines will help the owner select a consultant.

- On large, complex projects that require use of critical path method (CPM) scheduling, select an A/E who has demonstrated knowledge and experience of CPM. At the same time, avoid calling for such elaborate scheduling unless absolutely necessary. CPM is costly and misused on many occasions.
- Use local talent, if qualified. The benefits to be derived from this practice are many and include familiarity with local codes and utility companies, a factor of paramount importance.
- Select a firm that will commit its top personnel to the project in question. Too often, large firms are selected on the basis of their reputation. However, it is unrealistic to assume that the consultant is able to or will assign top talent to each project.
- Select the most qualified firm and then negotiate. Avoid using competitive bidding for professional services.
- Place equal emphasis on the selection of the engineering members of the team as on selection of the architects, even though contracts are most frequently written with the architect. Energy conservation, and operating and

23

maintenance costs especially, are worthy of the same design and layout. Over the life of the facility, operation and maintenance could cost more than seven times the original capital investment.

Design Priority Allocations. The design process is an area that deserves special emphasis, because it is at this stage that most problems can be solved. Design costs are minimal in comparison to the initial construction cost, as well as the operating and maintenance costs over the life of the building.

It is essential for the success of a project to allow sufficient time to create and review plans adequately, to rework design to minimize change orders associated with errors and omissions, and to research design concepts to ensure that they will work in the field. For the best results in design:

- Work closely with the A/E during the design process. Do "on-board" reviews as much as possible to save time that is normally lost in design review. A knowledgeable critique of the design can be very helpful to the consultant. A review by future maintenance personnel can be especially useful in assuring proper access to the equipment as well as adequate storage and custodial space.
- On large projects, employ a value engineering specialist to help review the design in the preliminary stages.
- Utilize the services of an outside professional cost estimator to provide accurate cost estimates at the design development and bid stage. This information is a valuable yardstick in meeting budgetary goals.

Bidding. Before bidding, take the time to review drawings and specifications as thoroughly as possible. Make a note of products that are available at competitive prices. "Approved equals" and "substitutions" should be avoided whenever possible. "Approved equals" means "or cheaper" to the general contractor; similarly, substitutions should not be allowed unless reasonable credit is given to the owner. To increase the likelihood of a successful bid:

- Prequalify bidders if possible. A contractor's references from previous jobs are valuable indicators of his capabilities. If it is feasible to pre-qualify contractors in this manner, it may not be necessary to request bid or performance bonds and the attendant costs can be avoided.
- Allow the bidders sufficient time to bid. Takeoffs on construction projects are cumbersome and take time. Moreover, if sufficient time is allotted to the general contractor, a greater number of quality bids can be expected, and competitive bids will be the result.
- Avoid "add or deduct" alternates. Generally, if these are included in the bid package, they will become added costs. Contractors include a greater contingency in their bids if the value of "add or deduct" alternates are significant.

Pre-Construction Meeting. Regular construction meetings should be established and held at least every two weeks. The consultant should be responsible for keeping minutes. Remember to:

- Meet with code, fire, and utility officials at the preliminary or schematic design phase, to avoid problems later in obtaining building permits.
- Discuss change order philosophy, bill paying, stored materials, shop drawing submittals, "substitutions/approved equals" submittals, safety, cleanup, quality control, outside testing, etc.

Construction. Construction supervision should not be taken lightly. Unless it is contracted for with the consultant, supervision is considered the owner's responsibility. Since construction is still considered an art, building exactly to plans and specifications doesn't happen without proper supervision by the owner. To streamline construction supervision:

- Interview the construction superintendent; he or she is the key to good construction.
- Take periodic photographs of construction progress. Add special photos as problems arise. Keep daily logs.
- Contract directly with steel, concrete, or soils-testing companies if you need these services. Avoid letting the contractor take charge of this phase.
- Try to solve problems as a team.
- Make decisions as rapidly as possible.
- Pay all bills on time both to the consultant and the contractors.
- Do not reduce retention unless you are satisfied that the contractor is making reasonable progress. It is recommended to hold back 10 percent of the amount due until the project is 75 percent complete, and then reduce it to 5 percent, provided reasonable progress is made. Except for the most extraordinary contractor, the retention should not be further reduced until "punch list" items are complete and all contract terms and conditions are satisfied.
- Enforce all specifications requirements including as built or record drawings, maintenance manuals, maintenance training, and maintenance contracts.

Post-Construction. The facilities manager stands to gain in the long run by keeping track of the project after completion. To follow up on the project:

- Request a written report from the consultants based on the first year's operation and use of the facility. Use this feedback as input for future projects.
- Encourage maintenance personnel to provide regular reports.

PREQUALIFYING A CONTRACTOR . . .
A MAJOR CONSTRUCTION DECISION

In any building program, the facilities manager's selection of the method of building, the architect-engineer—and certainly the best-qualified contractor—is very important.

It is the contractor, in the last analysis, whose activities determine the progress of the project within the allocated budget and time schedule. The guidelines presented here are intended to help the facilities manager in his prequalification of contractors; the forms are evaluation sheets and references check sheets to appraise potential bidders. We have used them successfully in our construction programs.

Before issuing specifications for a bid, a preliminary reference check should be made to ensure that the contractors invited to bid can purchase the materials and carry the payrolls required for the project. Each contractor's experience in the specific type of construction involved should be investigated, and in some cases, the proposed superintendents and key foremen should be interviewed.

Generally, large construction firms offer the advantages of experience in a broad range of building types; a small firm, however, may be especially competent in constructing the type of building being bid. And, large firms may have a lower-limit cutoff point for size of jobs they will accept, although this will vary with the location and nature of the assignment and the contractor's current commitments.

In our prequalification interview, we discuss the project and its specific requirements. We place considerable emphasis on schedule limitations; further, we explore financial strength, relationships with subcontractors and labor unions, current workload, business philosophy, etc. The contractor is informed that we will also interview his/her superintendent and the subcontractors' foreperson.

To assist us in filling out the qualification forms, we ask for a financial statement and an annual report. We check Dun & Bradstreet, the contractor's bank, his subcontractors, and fill in the Contractor Evaluation Form. To obtain the information for the Contractor Reference Check, we ask the contractor to list three of his recent projects that are similar in size and dollar volume to ours. The owners of these projects are then asked to help us rate the contractor.

On one of our projects, we used the accumulated data to rate the ten general contractors who had expressed a desire to bid. With our architect/engineer's help, we selected the four most qualified. These contractors were given the bid package with which they prepared their bids. After we obtained each contractor's bid, we supplemented his/her figures with our prequalification appraisal results, and were in an excellent position to select the one best contractor for our project.

Contractor's Reference Checks

DATE:_____

REFERENCE:

1. Did the contractor meet or exceed all of the major scheduled milestones?

2. Was the contract fixed price or cost-plus negotiated fee?

3. Did the contractor perform within the price quoted?

    A. Was there any evidence of material substitutions or other corner-cutting activities?

4. Were there any instances of delay caused by the lack of coordination between subcontractors or the unavailability of materials at the site when needed?

5. Did the contractor maintain a harmonious labor-management atmosphere?

6. To the best of your knowledge, did the contractor maintain a good working relationship with his subcontractors throughout the construction program?

7. Did the contractor maintain a harmonious community relationship during the program?

8. Are there any items appearing now as substandard in the building which can be attributed to the negligence of the contractor?

9. Was the assigned field superintendent sufficiently knowledgeable to adequately supervise the activities of all subcontractors, or was there some evidence of the subcontractors operating independently on their assigned portions of the program?

10. Did the contractor show a tendency towards overpricing customer requested changes?

11. What is your overall impression of his ability to perform major construction programs?

Contractor Evaluation

Name of Contractor:
Address:
Telephone Number:

Project for which evaluated:

Project Title	Location

I. General Background	Considerable Amount	Fair Amount	None
a. Experience in construction of this type facility	_____	_____	_____
b. Construction experience in general geographical area of proposed project	_____	_____	_____
c. Average value of projects handled	$ _____		
d. Average annual volume of work in place	$ _____		
e. Current workload (value of uncompleted work)	$ _____		

f. Able to undertake this project within normal workload

	Yes	No
	_____	_____

g. Financial strength (current tangible net worth) $ _____

h. Credit rating

	Ecellent	Good	Fair	Poor
	_____	_____	_____	_____

i. Stated interest in bidding this project

	Yes	No
	_____	_____

j. Has contractor successfully used critical path method (CPM) scheduling?

	Yes	No
	_____	_____

II. Project architect's recommendation (in order of preference of all contractors considered, after having completed performance ratings based on personal knowledge, and/or work performed under at least three (3) other clients and architects.

No. _____ of _____ evaluated.

(Attached performance rating sheets)

_____
Signature of Architect or
Architect's Representative

Performance rating based on (Architect's kowledge) and / or check with
(other clients) (other architects). Check as appropriate.

	Exc	Good	Fair	Poor
a. Top Management attention to project	____	____	____	____
b. Staffing of job to assure home office and field supervision, expediting and coordination of the work of all trades	____	____	____	____
c. Ability to meet construction schedules	____	____	____	____
d. Cooperation, speed and reasonableness in pricing and performing changes in the work	____	____	____	____
e. Promptness and completeness in submission of samples and shop drawings	____	____	____	____
f. Provision of materials of quality and quantity as called for in specifications and delivery of same on schedule	____	____	____	____
g. Selection of qualified and reputable material supplies and subcontractors	____	____	____	____
h. History of competitive bidding	____	____	____	____
i. Quality of workmanship	____	____	____	____
j. Maintenance of up-to-date as-built drawings	____	____	____	____
k. Maintenance of up-to-date records on schedule, material and cost	____	____	____	____
l. Cooperation with Owner and Architect	____	____	____	____
m. Promptness in payments to material suppliers and subcontractors	____	____	____	____
n. Overall performance rating	____	____	____	____

Rating based on:
1) Type of construction/facility   _____
2) Location of facility   _____
3) Dollar Value and Year $ _____

MINIMIZING MAINTENANCE COSTS
BY DESIGNING-IN MAINTAINABILITY
IN NEW OR EXPANDED FACILITIES

Maintenance problems begin while a building is being designed.
Most owners and consultants often overlook maintainability as a
major design criteria. The end result can be disastrous as far as
operations and maintenance are concerned. Including certain maintenance features in the design will pay for themselves many times
over during the life of the building.

With help from the company's maintenance operation or a
maintenance consultant firm, building owners should establish cer-

tain maintenance standards and specifications. The maintenance staff or consultant firm must also help review design drawings and specifications at various intervals. All too often, maintenance personnel get involved too late to do much good. They should participate from the very start.

The program of requirements for facilities today usually includes eliminating barriers for the handicapped as well as conforming to energy conservation and IAQ design criteria. Meeting these program objectives sometimes creates more problems since most state-of-the-art energy-conservative mechanical equipment is complex and requires more maintenance. Also, provisions for the handicapped usually require equipment that normally would not be needed and thus add to maintenance costs. With these requirements demanding more time and attention from the maintenance staff, it is important that all routine maintenance chores can be accomplished as efficiently as possible. Therefore, maintainability should be an important part of the program requirements.

Owner's Fault

If maintenance employees do not participate in the design process, many will complain about facets of the operation and blame the architect/consultant for problems that arise. In such cases, the architect/consultant is not to blame; the owner is. The owner is the manager of the design/consultant team, so the overall success of a capital project depends on his/her abilities, knowledge, and leadership.

In some respects, the consultant's role can be compared to that of a computer, the better the input, the better the output. The output in this case is in the form of construction documents which, when the facility is built, will last for forty or more years. To improve design from a maintainability standpoint the owner must make very clear to the designer the program of requirements relating to operation and maintenance of the new or expanded facility. Communication should be in writing so that misinterpretation is minimized.

The following checklist contains some of the areas that I have found to be troublesome during my 35 years of experience as an owner, responsible for design, construction, and maintenance. This list is by no means complete, but hopefully it will serve as an example that will help your company's building project.

Structural/Concrete/Masonry

- Sufficient expansion joints should exist in sidewalks and concrete floors to minimize cracking and replacement.
- In cold climates, depth of sidewalks should be sufficient to prevent heaving.
- Ramps to parking lots and entrances to buildings should have snow-melting embedded wiring.
- All curbs by roadways and parking areas should be concrete.
- Asphalt paving should have a more than adequate subbase and 2" topping.
- Asphalt paving in parking lots should be sealed to prevent deterioration from oil spills, salt, etc.
- The use of aggregate concrete finish on entrances and walks should be avoided if salt will be used as a snow removal agent or if a small plow will be utilized.
- Sidewalks should be located where people would normally walk. Symmetry of design is not the important criterion in location of walks.

Civil/Landscaping

- Landscaping should be kept simple to allow mechanized equipment to be used whenever possible. Don't include landscaped areas within parking lots unless you use ground cover that needs little maintenance. Also avoid extensive planting of flower beds.
- Sufficient, uncloggable roof drains, scuppers, interior and exterior storm drains should be incorporated.

- Outside receptacles and hose bibs should be carefully planned and freeze-protected.
- Outdoor storage for grounds maintenance equipment should be considered.
- Detailed attention should be given to swale design.

Mechanical

- Tight air balancing specs need to be developed.
- Filters, filter racks and monitoring equipment should be carefully studied. The contractor should provide new filters at occupancy.
- Proper ventilation and additional A/C should be considered for all major conference areas.
- Access to valves and other equipment should be provided.
- Mounting of heavy equipment should be on concrete pads with shock absorbers that will minimize vibration and provide acoustic control.
- Air intake locations need to be carefully studied to avoid fumes, dust and dirt.
- Controls should be digital, appropriate for the type of equipment specified.
- Zones—numbers of zones should be stated.

Electrical

- Energy-efficient lighting should be a standard. Establish the lighting level desired (as little as 1 W/SF). Study the use of perimeter photoelectric controls and task lighting. Look for maintenance features that will facilitate access to lamps for changing.
- Access to lighting (i.e., scaffolds, ladders, etc.) is important.
- Spare capacity should be included on main switchboard. Panels need to be properly identified.
- Access to space or conduit should be placed to permit expansion.

- Switchgear and other major electrical equipment should be of excellent quality.
- Ensure that power for PCs is clean and conditioned.
- Use of four-plex outlets should be directed at desk locations.
- Ground fault and other safety protection should be specified.
- Secondary power sources should exist.
- Emergency power requirements should be studied carefully.
- Special installations such as computers and laboratories must be designed carefully.
- Spare parts should be available.
- Motor thermal overload protection is desirable (three phases).
- Receptacles should be placed in hallways/stairwells for ease of vacuuming and other maintenance purposes.
- Aluminum wiring should be avoided wherever possible.

Roof

- Quality design and construction is imperative. Request pitched roofs wherever possible and give as much attention to the roof as to other parts of the building.
- Penetrations and perimeter treatment of roof (use of scuppers) should be studied carefully.
- Sufficient roof drains should be incorporated.

Telephone

- Extra wide/deep underfloor ducts should be installed to facilitate any anticipated moves and expansion.
- Closets should have plywood facing where needed as well as electrical receptacles for telephone equipment.
- Placement of closets is important.

Ceilings

- Panels should be removable—either 2' x 2' or 2' x 4' and marked when piping/valving is overhead.

Carpentry

- Acoustics of closed offices should be specified.
- Although ½" dry wall is generally used as a standard, 5/8" should be utilized.
- Hardware schedule approval should be coordinated with maintenance.

Painting/Wall Surfaces

- Paint specs should require a prime coat and two coats using an excellent quality paint.
- Semi-enamel or an equally washable paint on all surfaces should be specified.
- Public corridors should be applied with heavy duty vinyl wall covering (excluding lobby, where even more durable finishes may be desired).

Entrances/Exits

- Double vestibules with "dirt-catching" floor surfaces should be incorporated in the design.

Windows

- Opening, double-insulated windows should be considered for ventilation in certain seasons and for cleaning. Key windows so that only maintenance personnel can open them.
- Sills should be sloped to prevent water retention. Sloped sills also discourage pigeons and other birds from roosting.

- Windowshades and other energy features should be incorporated in the design. Drapery pockets should be provided where drapes will be used.

Restrooms

- Small closets should be included for convenient storage of restroom maintenance materials.
- Ceramic tile should be used for walls and floors. Ceilings should be painted dry wall or metal (semi-gloss paint).
- Fixtures and toilet partitions should be wall hung.
- Sinks, water closets and urinals accessible to the handicapped are required.
- Drains should be specified in each restroom.
- Adequate ventilation and properly placed lighting are important.
- Proper access to chase.
- Tempered hot water, single faucet sinks should be considered.
- Width and placement of doors must be considered carefully (privacy and access).
- Drinking fountains should be self-contained, which is generally better for handicapped persons and maintenance.

Custodial

- Adequate main storage for custodial equipment and supplies is essential.
- Well-designed custodial closets with slop sink and receptacle are useful.

Trash

- Trash room should use compactors if possible.
- If dumpsters are used, access, placement and screening are design considerations.

- Trash flow patterns to disposal areas should be carefully studied to ensure best placement of trash room/dumpsters.

Storage

- Storage areas for inactive files and maintenance supplies should be included in program of requirements.

Carpeting

- Carpet seams should be minimized. Glued down commercial grade carpeting is generally best in 12" widths.
- Carpet with an acceptable flame spread rating is essential. All carpet should be thoroughly clean upon acceptance of building.

Maintenance Materials/Training

- Sufficient number of copies of maintenance manuals should be ordered.
- Maintenance personnel should visit construction site to become familiar with the facility and provide feedback during construction.
- Lead mechanic should be stationed on site for 2-3 months prior to occupancy to become familiar with systems.
- Consultants and mechanical/electrical contractor should train all maintenance personnel on the proper operation and maintenance (including preventive maintenance) of equipment. Training should be conducted both in classroom and on-site and captured on video.

Record Drawings

- Sepias should be required so that drawings can be reproduced when needed.

Elevators

- Cab sizes, speeds, finishes and quality specifications should be given to consultant for incorporation into the design. Give special consideration to freight elevators.

Coffee/Vending Areas

- Policy should be established to limit areas within a building for this type of activity. These areas should feature durable, washable finishes and be well ventilated.

Copiers

- Ensure that copier receptacles and supplemental A/C are provided.

Standardization

- Equipment and materials specified should be similar to existing buildings to minimize stocking as well as to provide better, more efficient maintenance.

Maintenance Area

- Proper locker and shower facility for maintenance personnel should be provided.
- Maintenance room should be provided as required.
- Separate areas in mechanical rooms/penthouses should be set aside as work space (e.g. for stand-up desk, tool storage, spare parts).

Testing

- Maintenance personnel should be present when all mechanical and electrical systems are tested.

5

A STEP-BY-STEP APPROACH TO SUCCESSFUL PROJECT MANAGEMENT

Many facility managers are responsible for managing projects in the areas of new and retrofit design and construction, maintenance and energy conservation. A project is a concerted effort defined by a scope of services, schedule and costs.

The following is a step-by-step checklist that can help ensure that your projects run more smoothly with minimal complications.

Initially, it is important to understand that management and project management have different objectives. The objective of management is to stay in business for the longest period of time. The objective of project management is to complete the project and be "out of business" in the shortest period of time. Projects are the lifeblood of most companies. They are the parts that make up the whole, defined as management. (See Figure 1) How well each project does determines how successful a company will be in any given year.

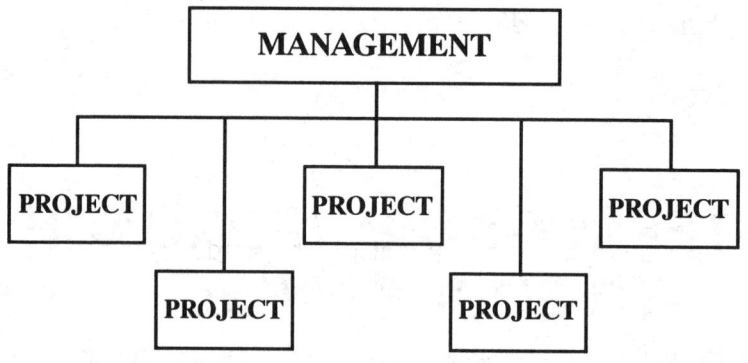

FIGURE 1

Management and project management have different objectives. The objective of management is to stay in business for the longest period of time. The objective of project management is to complete the project and be "out of business" in the shortest period of time. Projects are the parts that make up the whole, defined as management.

Usually facilities management departments are considered overhead by top management and generally don't get the recognition they deserve. Without much work on your part, you can reverse that opinion by indicating project-by-project savings or minimized costs. Management can easily relate to this and begin recognizing you and your department's contributions. After all, every dollar saved in overhead falls directly to the bottom line.

The biggest risk to a successful project is delay. More than any other single factor, delay will impact performance in a negative manner. Soaring construction costs and missed deadlines are usually the effects of delay. Consider any and all delays as the most formidable enemies of a successful project.

Because delays are often caused by oversights, disorganization, and miscommunications, the key elements of management—planning, organizing, directing (leading) and controlling—must be consciously utilized in managing projects. Objectives must be set in writing, a plan must be developed to meet the objectives, and a method must be determined to measure progress. The plan should be in writing in order to promote team effort, communicate to team members, provide visibility and confidence, and serve as a standard of performance.

There are various techniques that can be used in project management. These include work breakdown statements, schedules, reports, progress meetings, action item lists, periodic reviews with management involvement, and accounting system reports. Although these are integral parts of managing projects, they don't guarantee success. The manner in which a project is managed by the individual will have significant impact on the success or failure of a given project.

Successful project management requires attention to detail with continual follow-through on real or potential problems that may arise.

Let us assume you are working as a project manager for a general contractor. Your company has just executed a contract with a client for a fixed sum and the project has to be complete in a given period of time. You have just been delegated responsibility and authority to manage this project. The following checklist shows some of the steps that must be taken to ensure success.

Job Familiarization

1. Read the job file thoroughly, reviewing the contract and scope of services or plans/specifications. Use a headliner to highlight major points.
2. Visit the job site.
3. Meet all players.
4. Attend a job kick-off meeting led by estimating personnel.

Other attendees should be field personnel (job superintendent) and purchasing agents. The purpose of the meeting is
to review in detail the manner in which the job was esti-
mated and to highlight equipment that requires long-lead
times for ordering.

5. Set up and man the job. Arrange for a field office and materials storage trailer, telephone service, and trash service.
Post required notices (OSHA, safety, workmen's compen-
sation) and apply for permits.

6. Set up project files with separate sections for correspondence, subcontracts, purchase orders, change orders, accounting reports, progress payments and billings.

Pre-Construction

7. Attend pre-construction meetings with the client. These
meetings set ground rules, define various responsibilities
and provide opportunities to ask questions.

8. Buy out the project. Conclude negotiations and finalize
written contracts with subcontractors and suppliers. Order
all equipment/materials that involve long lead times.

9. Review project buy-out with estimates for each line item.
Meet with accounting personnel to develop project reporting system. Very rarely will the buy-out be in sync with the
estimate and it is important to relate progress against the
buy-out after the project has been bought out.

10. Prepare and present a written construction schedule to the
client.

11. Prepare a schedule of values by work category for billing to
client. Have it reviewed and accepted by client prior to any
billing.

12. Prepare list of subcontractors and major suppliers for client.

13. Prepare necessary submittals and shop drawings required by
plans/specifications and submit to client (via A/E).

Construction

14. Attend progress meetings. Take minutes of meetings and have them typed and distributed by the following day. Highlight action items and follow-up on each. The importance of follow-up cannot be overemphasized.
15. Ensure that the job is being coordinated properly, is properly manned, is clean and safe, and stays on schedule.
16. Review job superintendent's daily diary regarding manning.
17. Have photographs taken periodically.
18. Ensure that time sheets are completed properly and in a timely and accurate manner.
19. Coordinate with the A/E regarding field problems as they develop.
20. Review accounting reports on a timely basis and make necessary changes to keep project cost under control.
21. Do not proceed with any change orders unless directed and authorized in writing by the proper individual. Price out changes immediately.
22. Communicate with client in writing as much as possible. Significant telephone conversations should be followed up in writing. An example: "Per our telecon, this is to confirm your oral directions ...." A paper trail of your decisions, instructions, and actions minimizes confusion as a project develops, leaves no doubt as to what was communicated, and usually averts lawsuits.
23. Insist on quality work from all parties.
24. Ensure that billings are submitted on time and reviewed with the client prior to sending them out. Follow up with client on any late payments.
25. Pay invoices to subcontractors/suppliers within contract terms and conditions.
26. Plan for project close out.
    - prepare operating/maintenance manuals;
    - prepare punch lists and complete all items on a timely basis;
    - arrange for testing/balancing;

- provide written guarantees/warranties to client;
- gather up spare parts/materials and give them to client;
- arrange for start-ups of equipment;
- train client personnel;
- prepare as-built plans;
- assist client in arranging service agreements.

These steps are necessary to close out a project properly and to expedite retention reduction.

27. Send thank-you letter to client.
28. Arrange for post-construction meeting with client six months after project completion.
29. Write a final project report, including final financial results. Share the information with estimating.

Following the twenty-nine steps above can help you carry out your next project in a planned and well-organized manner. Attention to detail coupled with continual follow-up will help you get the project wrapped up and out-of-business as fast as possible.

The checklist can also help you get off to a fast start, which is important, because first impressions are lasting impressions.

6

THE HIDDEN COSTS
OF LEASING

Reengineering the Leasing Process

The average successful company doubles its office space every five years. Leasing commercial space and dealing with the consequences has become a major part of the facilities management profession. Analyzing a total lease cost on the surface appears easy, but it is very difficult and complex because you never have the time to obtain all the information you need to make an educated decision. Proper time for planning is *essential* to the process and there is no looking back once a lease is executed.

All too often, tenants become disappointed with their space after being in the space for only a short while and become even more frustrated and regret their decision after the first year, when they become shocked with exorbitant operating expense pass-throughs and other hidden costs of leasing which they did not budget for. Their dilemma does not end. They also become dejected when the services they expect don't materialize and especially when they experience temperature control problems and a host of other mechanical/plumbing breakdowns caused by poor maintenance. And, finally they get down-right "scared" when employees begin to miss work, and point at poor indoor air quality (IAQ) as the culprit. Poor IAQ results from poor maintenance.

During the years 1989 through 1997 there has been more space on the market than could be absorbed and vacancy rates soared. Many buildings foreclosed and were later bought at bargain prices by entrepreneurs, and the real estate primary players changed. The real estate market today is 80% third party management and 20% asset ownership. What this means is that pension funds and other investors came on the scene and own the majority of real estate in the U.S. with a philosophy of maximizing their investments by decreasing their operating expenses and increasing net operating income (NOI), usually at the expense of tenants. Or, the purchaser became an instant developer with an objective of giving the building a "cosmetic makeover" in order to lease up the space and then sell it at a substantial profit soon after it was fully leased.

During this time period, tenants were able to negotiate a great deal on rent and accepted buildings that were not being maintained properly and whose infrastructures were deteriorating. Another compounding problem were the building managers or management companies, who accepted bonuses and contract performance provisions based on reducing building expenses even further.

The cycle is now changing. Vacancy rates are low because construction of new commercial office space slowed drastically during recent years and the economy has improved. Owners are beginning to enjoy higher rental rates, to see healthy NOI's materialize, and starting to spend money on the building infrastructure, which will result in escalating operating expenses and "alarming" lease pass throughs to the unsuspecting tenant. The escalating operating expenses will come at the same time as the higher rental rates and real estate taxes. And, maintenance staffs, which have been downsized and reengineered drastically are not being increased, so do not expect to see upgrades in service levels or good maintenance.

What can you do about it? Learn to buy smart. By this I mean, take the time to obtain the information you need before executing any lease, riders, amendments and lease renewal. Regarding the latter, start negotiating two years prior to the time you need to make a decision and look at several sites so that the Landlord knows you are serious about negotiating a lease extension. Also, get help up front from a real estate consultant or tenant broker to assist you in gathering the information you need in plenty of time to make an informed decision.

Checklists for gathering important information are included as part of this chapter. Paying as much attention to the building's infrastructure and how well it is maintained is as important as the aesthetic qualities that have always been weighed heavily by Tenants in making lease decisions. Look more carefully at the elevators; type, age and condition of mechanical equipment; restrooms; plumbing; quality of and staffing of maintenance; on-site property management; core factor; how space is measured; operating costs for each building; parking; conference/meeting space available; ADA accessibility; cleaning specifications; maintenance performance specifications; security; indoor air quality; windows; building envelope; solar shading; expansion capability; etc. The results of this type of evaluation will pleasantly surprise you and all parties to the process will win because there will be a more thorough understanding of the lease, expectations will be realized and employees will be happier. All buildings are different and it is important to be able to identify the differences. Let's examine just a few of these.

On-site Management

Is there an on-site manager on premises and how do you judge a good one from a bad one? Is he/she "qualified" or do they just collect rent? Does the firm have a facility manager on staff? If so, interview both the Facility Manager, Property Manger and Chief Engineer and ask for a list of all subcontracts in the building and their performance standards.

There is nothing more frustrating than dealing with an "off-site", buck-passing landlord who will not answer his/her phone when desperately needed.

Operating Expenses

Very seldom do these clauses favor tenants. In fact, they do the opposite. Ask the developer to break down operating expenses in detail. Do they include taxes, marketing, broker fees, tenant improvement costs, security, cleaning, financing for capital expenses? You should also know that newer buildings have lower tax assessments which can be bumped significantly when the building gets occupied. Also, remember that first-year operating costs are always very low, especially in new buildings, because of guarantees and warranties on equipment and material. Once these expire, you will face a significant jump in operating expenses.

Core Factor and Space

The space leased includes useable space, rentable space, and a core factor. Rentable space includes common areas and service facilities. Useable space is the space you actually use for your offices. The core factor is the difference between rentable and useable space. Examine blueprints carefully. If the "core" of the building is central, then you will probably benefit from a low core factor. But if the core is spread out, you can anticipate a problem.

Ask the developer how space will be measured and you measure it. You will always come up with a lower number (that shouldn't surprise you). It's not the cost/SF in leasing that counts, it's the amount of space. And, did you know that the developer measures to the inside of windows? Often this will include the actual width of the walls, individual HVAC units and columns that cannot be utilized by your layout.

Power/Lighting Availability

Check into space available for electrical/communication cabling in risers and above ceilings. Examine electrical closets and check electrical power panels for spare capacity and transformers. If the building is older (circa 1978 and before) the building's transformers could create a harmonics problem and interfere with your computing systems. And ask about electrical loads? Sophisticated land-lords allow about 5 watts/SF in a lease and meter all spaces. The high-tech office of today may use 7-8 watts/SF (including tradi-tional lighting loads).

Also check the building to see if high efficiency lighting is avail-able, such as deep-cell parabolic lighting and what that design load is. This could reduce utility costs by over 40%. If the landlord in-vests in high efficiency lighting after you've moved in, guess who pays for the investment, the tenant, and who gets the added value of the asset, the landlord!

Parking

Parking is often taken for granted but it is an important consid-eration. Developers concerned with short-term cash flow often overlook the need for good parking. In fact they use minimal stan-dards and cut maintenance to the core.

How many spaces will be available for you? How wide are they? What is the ratio of covered/open space parking? What is the condition of the surface treatment—is it well maintained, striped and well lighted? How far do your employees have to walk? Is it safe? Can you park a car easily? Do columns in garages jut out to create problems in parking? How many reserved spaces can you have? Where are they in the garage? Is the garage well maintained and well ventilated? Is it clean and safe? Who does the cleaning? Are the building's air intake grilles close to parking areas?

Security

Better buildings offer 24-hour guard service, including roving guards during off hours. The service should be provided by reputa-ble companies. Added security and safety is offered through access control (including elevators), motion detectors, and cameras.

HVAC/Plumbing

HVAC issues have headed the list of tenant complaints for years and with the undersized maintenance staffs in buildings today, it is recommended that you conduct an evaluation of the mechanical systems and the operating/maintenance program prior to leasing or renewing leases. Considering the growing numbers of indoor air quality lawsuits alone would support the recommendation of having IAQ checked out thoroughly beforehand. 80% of IAQ problems could be solved if good maintenance were the norm, but the simple truth is that buildings are not being maintained well and poor IAQ results.

A lease can be negotiated and written as much from the tenant's view as from the landlord's but only watchful shoppers avoid paying owners undue — and often hidden — profits. And in every case, call existing tenants and ask them whether or not they are satisfied and what they have experienced with their lease.

OTHER LEASING TIPS

- Measure space
- Call tenants for references
- Have consultants evaluate mechanical systems and audit operating/maintenance costs for candidate buildings
- Find out how the building is operated (is it union/non-union)
- Review the ENTIRE lease and negotiate ALL clauses
- Review rules and regulations
- Watch timing — is it realistic?
- Make sure that you know your rights
- Have experts review the lease analyses
- Once a lease is signed, it's too late

Sample Leasing Data Form

LOCATION:
- Image
- Traffic
- Neighbors
- Mail Delivery
- Eating facilities
- Public transportation
- Available recreation
- Other services nearby

BUILDING:
- Elevators (#, size)
- Freight elevators
- Loading dock
- Parking (#, cost)
    - width of spaces
- Reserved parking
- Covered parking
- Visitors parking
- Handicapped parking
- Landscaping
- Stories
- Area per floor
- Net rentable sq. ft.
- Lobby (sq. ft.)
- Rest rooms
- Power availability
- Mechanical system (type, age, maintenance)
    - indoor air quality
    - solar shading
    - EMS available
- Individual controls in office
- Windowed offices
- Appearance & general maintenance
- Char Service
    - Quality
- On-site engineers, property manager
- Quality of maintenance program

- Security
  — 24 hour
- Operating hours; after hours use (cost)
- High efficiency lighting available
- Telecommunications network
- Signage permitted
- Rules & regulations
- Age of building
- Standard finishes

LEASING INFORMATION:

- Sq. Ft. available
  — Expansion (right of first   refusal)
- Exposure (N, E, S, W)
- Base rent
- Additional rent:
  — CPI
  — Operating expenses
  — Taxes
  — Insurance
  — Supplemental air conditioning
  — Utilities
- Obtain:
  — Copy of standard lease
  — Standard work letter
  — Unit prices for tenant improvements
- Core factor
- Base term
- Expandability
- Options available
- How will sq. ft. in lease be determined?
- Lease commencement date
- Rent commencement date
- Is interior design available in rent?
- How will acceptance of premises be determined?
- How will pass-throughs be determined?
  — Base year
  — (Negotiate this clause in all cases since in the initial year the building in all probability will not be fully occupied)

7

EXCELLENCE IN FACILITIES MANAGEMENT

Moving from the Back Office to the Executive Office

Productivity through people will become the difference maker in the twenty-first century and employers will continue to expand without hiring additional full-time employees, reaching their objectives by both skill-set training and mind set-training. Reliance on technical competence alone will leave many facilities managers behind to manage things and projects, while those who proactively and progressively seek added training in business skills and people skills will move on to higher management positions in the company.

Today's employers need strong leaders who:

- have and maintain a positive attitude
- adapt fast
- "buy in" and embrace change
- have a sense of urgency
- cooperate well with others
- accept ambiguity and uncertainty
- behave as if it were their own business
- keep on learning
- are self motivated
- motivate by example

- hold themselves accountable
- aren't afraid to make mistakes
- add value; i.e., contribute much more than they cost
- get close to their customers
- continuously improve
- are solutions-oriented, not finger pointers
- develop positive, caring workplaces
- mentor and contribute to the growth of others
- know how to communicate and communicate often, face to face

PRODUCTIVITY THROUGH PEOPLE

Many of these needs described above are generally weaknesses found in facilities managers, who have excellent technical skills but possess below average interpersonal skills and business skills, especially in the finance area. So, we must develop the skills needed to reinforce our weaknesses in order to move from a supportive role to a leadership role. We have too many managers in our profession and not enough leaders–people who are committed to grow others and help them reach their full potential.

What lies ahead of us are both opportunities and challenges, unlike anything we've faced before. Recognizing that we must become more productive and more growth is achievable in productivity through people than in any other way, we should concentrate on further reinforcing our people skills. And, recognizing that facilities management is a financially based business (everything that we do involves money), we should be communicating more often with top management in terms that they more easily understand; e.g., return on investment (ROI), savings, income statement, cash flow, balance sheets, opportunity cost, life cycle cost analysis, pro-formas, inventory control, etc. Educating management, developing positive, caring environments, thinking like a chief financial officer, and focusing on improving the image of our maintenance operations can go a long way toward attaining our goal of moving up in the organization chart in the quickest way possible.

IMPROVING THE IMAGE OF MAINTENANCE

Thirty-five years ago maintenance represented 0.7% of revenues. Today maintenance represents between 9.5 and 15% of revenues. Although many facilities management organizations have responsibility for strategic planning, design and construction of buildings, operating and maintaining buildings and grounds have always been the mainstay of facilities management. The image of operations and maintenance in most organizations is poor. Productivity is low (25-35%) and maintenance departments have been traditionally seen as inefficient and ineffective, except in emergencies. Staffs have been poorly trained and unappreciated by management, who look upon this function as an expense, but not as a contributor to the bottom line.

This perception may very well be a myth, but it is a very real perception to many in the work place. This poor image has had a negative effect on facility managers who often turn their back on what very well may be the best opportunity for improvement that they have. Rather than accepting mediocrity from their maintenance function, a facility manager should increase the expectation levels and focus on productivity improvements in maintenance.

Normally, maintenance staffs don't experience much turnover and consequently have a great deal of tenure, which makes them very expensive to retain over time (without equal or greater improvement in productivity). Also staffs have become unbalanced over time; i.e., maintenance personnel became skilled and with few replacements being hired in the 1990s, most maintenance organizations became top heavy with skilled mechanics and no apprentices or helpers. Outsourcing companies soon discovered an opportunity to provide an alternative through contracting out and approached CEOs and CFOs with less expensive ways to perform a function they didn't appreciate anyway. In the transition, many maintenance middle managers lost their jobs due to outsourcing, leaving behind a significant gap for mentoring younger employees.

LACK OF LEADERSHIP

The reason this has occurred is lack of leadership in facilities management by managers who were caught off guard and did little to prevent downsizing and outsourcing from happening. The poor image of maintenance is a direct reflection on the quality of our leadership in the 1990s.

Much can be done to improve the image and performance of the maintenance function such as:

- establishing and implementing a comprehensive maintenance and replacement program
- using computerized maintenance management systems and energy management systems
- establishing and implementing a preventive maintenance program where 90% of the preventive maintenance (PM) work orders issued get accomplished each month
- establishing and implementing a predictive maintenance program that will enhance service life of actual equipment
- developing a comprehensive labor plan and scheduling which includes
  – use of multi-skilled craftspersons
  – use of cross-training
- increasing use of contract maintenance, which is cost effective, to augment in-house efforts
- using established benchmarks for measuring maintenance performance
- developing sales strategies (which includes ROI) for replacing equipment
- separating renovations, remodeling, and alteration work from maintenance

- increasing expectations for all employees by concentrating on the human element (feelings, relationships and attitudes)
- establishing maintenance standards, involving employees in the process of implementing these strategies
- developing appropriate training programs to strengthen technical, financial and people skills of all service providers
- establishing a customer service/help desk
- developing a customer service handbook
- educating top management continually on improvements made in maintenance and the value provided by a well-trained maintained staff, expressing value in cost savings or productivity gains affecting the bottom line

DEFINITION OF MAINTENANCE

The definition of maintenance is *"to keep or preserve in an existing condition, in a state of efficiency or good repair."* What that should mean to top management is that good maintenance provides value, since it preserves our assets. Good maintenance pays for itself by reducing energy costs; by improving performance of equipment, extending life of the equipment by as much as 50%; less repairs; good indoor air quality (IAQ); and better safety. An even bigger consideration is that good maintenance increases capacity of production (less downtime of production lines), and when selling the asset, more money. Most facilities with energy management (EM) and computerized maintenance management (CMM) systems have reduced operating costs and increased productivity significantly while increasing the value of the asset.

WHAT LEADERSHIP BRINGS

Couple good maintenance management with the products of good leadership—high morale, a positive, caring workplace, happy people who always are more productive and miss less time, an energized and motivated workforce, and good communication, and you'll experience amazing results, as much as 100:1 ROI.

Good leaders will educate top management and champion causes that will elevate the image of their department. They also have the ability to educate and sell their ideas and projects that heretofore were deferred. Progressive facility leaders utilize video cameras and recorders with appropriate story lines, visual aids and charts, and a lot of financial data in order to present and sell their ideas to upper management.

Good leaders develop response teams, customer service representatives and help desks, and customer handbooks that enable customers to obtain service easier and quicker. And, good facility leaders commit themselves to *team excellence*, demanding a cooperative and expeditious search for the right "yes" by:

- seeking opportunity in all proposals
- working cooperatively with colleagues to find common purpose
- building on trust and mutual respect
- striving for excellence

Improving your leadership skills and the image of your maintenance operation will pay big dividends to your personal career and to our profession at large. Maintenance managers often complain about accounting managers and vice versa. I recently read the following in a trade journal, "Many people in top management, the bean counters as we call them, only see the maintenance department as a place that spends money." This illustrates the problem well. It looks like we have quite a bit of work to do in communicating, educating and working with our colleagues to meet the requirements of *team excellence*, to turn that image around and work cooperatively and positively forward. I say "we" because leaders generally make poor followers. If you aren't the lead dog, the view never changes.

SAVINGS THROUGH

Lighting Efficiency
 2.5 W/SF —> 1 W/SF
 40% reduction in utilities up to $1/SF

Chiller Efficiency
 Replacement/Conversion/Containment
 .8 KW —> .5 KW
 200 T - 300 T = $1,000/MO.

MAINTAIN (mán-tán') - to keep
**or preserve in an existing condition, in a
state of efficiency or good repair.**

GOOD MAINTENANCE MAKES SENSE

- Saves energy (10-15% of utilities costs)
- Maximizes good IAQ (80% of IAQ problems eliminated)
- PMM saves 60% of the cost of breakdown/corrective maintenance
- PMM extend life of equipment as much as 50%
- Contracted maintenance (to quality contractors) is much more efficient (about 30%) and always less expensive . . . . Albert Ramond & Associates
- Less repairs
- Better safety
- Improves performance of equipment
- Increases capacity of production
- Increases value of the asset
- Lowers total costs for O/M

8

DEVELOPING A FACILITIES MANAGEMENT SERVICE STRATEGY

One of the most important things an organization can do is determine exactly what business it is in.

— Peter Drucker

Facilities management is a financially based business that provides service, and as such, should try to differentiate itself by developing a strong reputation for delighting customers - beginning with its own employees. The service strategy should include the following elements:

Excellent Customer Service	Create A Welcoming Environment
	Create a Positive, Caring and Hassle-Free Environment
	Create an Informative Environment
	Without Forgetting to Be Efficient and Effective

How you do these things is important and will establish a style unique to your department.

CREATE A WELCOMING ENVIRONMENT

In a welcoming environment, all staff members act as if they personally own the company. Just as you would if you were hosting a party in your home, you should acknowledge each guest's presence as quickly as possible. Let your guests know that you are pleased to serve them and use their name whenever possible to let them know you care about them as individuals.

Appearance is important and you should expect all staff members to be well groomed and wear clean uniforms and a badge. Keep everything, including yourself, vans, work areas, and breakrooms clean and organized. Excelling in cleanliness is one of the best ways to create a welcoming environment. It shows how much you care about the work you do.

Welcome new employees into their new department by introducing them to their new environment in a caring, helpful manner. This makes them feel important and eager to start their new job. Develop an employee orientation notebook and personalized instructions to fully explain ethics, corporate values, corporate history, company mission, vision, employee benefits, policies and procedures, the organization chart, quality expectations, available training, and requirements for cleanliness and safety. Take new employees on a tour of the facility and introduce the employee to as many supervisors, fellow employees and customers as you can during his/her first days. For one month, assign a "buddy," a fellow employee who will ensure that the new employee's questions and concerns are satisfied and make him/her feel enthusiastic about their new job. All new employees should feel welcome and know exactly how they fit into the organization.

A welcoming environment for customers could be created in a similar manner. A customer service handbook and open orientation meetings on how to obtain caring and hassle-free services from facilities management will help immensely. Make it easy and fun for your internal customers to work with you. You should also establish a customer help desk staffed by your most helpful, friendly employees to take service requests and to answer any questions or handle any complaints by your customers. This shows that you welcome input, are problem-solvers and are there to help these customers do a better job. You can also help others by anticipating their needs and provide a means to satisfy their personal needs while at work. Some examples are on-site employee services including convenience stores that would provide ATM services, laundry, photo developing, small locker facilities, over- the-counter drugs, flowers, greeting cards and other essential personal times. Make it easy as possible for employees to enjoy their facility—both their work stations and the services areas.

CREATE A POSITIVE, CARING AND HASSLE-FREE ENVIRONMENT

You can create a caring and hassle-free environment by focusing on quality. In the service business, quality is defined as *"conformance to requirements–the customer's requirements."* All of your processes and systems should be designed to serve the customer.

Once customers' needs are established, the processes developed to do business with you should be easy to use and customer friendly. Review all your current policies and procedures in this manner and when you encounter problems, find and fix the root cause of the problem. Customer complaints are opportunities to find out what's wrong and correct it in a manner where it can't happen again. Once you've got the system right, the result should be right every time and you will achieve the quality standard you want : *to do the job right every time.*

Four Ways to Demonstrate Caring

Our customers want services to be of high quality *and* they want to be cared about and treated well. You could demonstrate caring as follows:

1. Friendly Service. Friendly service means more than courtesy. Customers want to feel as though their needs are important–that *they* are important. This means being interested, answering the phone quickly, giving information, listening carefully and answering questions and concerns. It also includes warm, friendly responses at all times, and especially when customers are upset or have some concerns.

2. Flexibility. When the service delivery system isn't meeting their needs, customers want the person who helps them to "tweak" the system to make it work for them. Customers don't want to hear "no." They want you to expeditiously search for the right "yes" and to figure out a way to get them what they want or need.

3. Problem Resolution. There are two parts to this. First, when customers have business problems that need some attention, they want to know that you will help them find a solution, even if you can't handle it yourself. For example, they want to know that they will not be transferred somewhere else and left with the responsibility for starting over and explaining their problem to someone else.

Second, they want you to respond to their non-business problems. For example, a customer with a flat tire in your parking lot wants you to do something for them—call a towing company or help in some way.

4. Recovery. When a mistake is made, customers want it to be taken care of quickly and to their satisfaction. They want some kind of action that recognizes a mistake has been made and every effort is being made to correct it. *When you "recover," you may find that your customer is even more loyal than before.*

Creating a caring and hassle-free environment is critical in developing a loyal base of customers. Customers expect you to meet their requirements 100% of the time. When you do not, you create a barrier to their loyalty. You cannot have loyal customers when your products and services do not meet their expectations. Even when you do meet their expectations, however, you will not automatically create loyal customers. You must create a caring environment as well.

CREATE AN INFORMATIVE ENVIRONMENT

Keeping everyone up-to-date on all types of information is important and challenging. Poor communication is always the number one complaint between employer and employees, and, people want to be involved and in the know of what's happening. By the same token, customers expect the service provider to keep them informed as much as possible in regard to the status of their work/service requests. Regarding the latter, often the customer is not there when the work is performed. To solve this problem, a preprinted sticky-back note that informs the customer that you were there and what was done can be used and left at the work station.

Complete Building Services

☐ Your request for service was completed.
☐ No one was available, I will try again later.

Service requested: _____

_____

Engineer: _____ Date: _____

The Ritz-Carlton Hotel company begins each day, and each shift, with what they call a "daily line-up"–short, ten-minute meetings to cover what's important that day to keep everyone "in the know." Try this, as well as weekly breakfast meetings on Mondays with supervisors to review plans for the week. Encourage staff to express any concern they have at an appropriate time during the meeting and also encourage employees to create new ideas for improving communication. Since we live in a diversified society, it may be a good idea for employees who speak a foreign language to wear a miniature flag pin on their name badge which corresponds to the language they speak.

Other communication tools used successfully are semi-annual excellence seminars for both employees and customers and semi-annual orientation sessions with administrative coordinators of other departments to answer questions they may have and to obtain feedback on your services. These workshops should be approximately four hours in length and basically address three questions:

- What do we do well today?
- What could we do better to serve you?
- What changes can we make to meet your goals?

After getting this feedback, prepare and distribute minutes of these sessions quickly and hold another similar follow-up meeting six months later to discuss results. This essentially will be your report card and feedback mechanism from both your employees and your internal customers. Start the process again the following month with different participants.

Another good feedback mechanism, especially for those facilities management organizations providing services to external customers, is to have your dispatch staff supervisors and customer service help desk staff regularly call customers and ask, "how are we doing?" and then, follow up by asking "were you satisfied with our service?". The results from the above should be shared with everyone involved, including letters of commendation that come into the office.

Lastly, sending a thank-you note to employees and customers expressing your appreciation for their business, consideration, follow-up, promptness, quality workmanship, or whatever will not only be thoughtful on your part but also a good way to make others feel important. It will cement good relationships, build morale and build business.

FOCUS ON THE EMPLOYEE

Companies are only as good as their employees and employees respond to their customers in exactly the same manner as they are treated. Employee satisfaction is measured by how much they look forward to coming to work every day and how important they feel.

If employees are happy, customers generally will be happy with the services they provide and better attendance will be the natural by-product.

Employee focus groups will give us the feedback we need and employee questionnaires should be designed to obtain feedback on the following factors:

- competent and effective supervision
- clear goals and objectives from the department
- safe and secure working conditions
- adequate pay and working conditions
- quick, responsive answers to problems
- welcome work environment
- informative work environment
- caring and hassle-free environment
- opportunity to learn and grow on the job
- opportunity for promotion (based on merit)
- positive social climate
- justice and fair play

In addition, managers should pay close attention and monitor accurate paychecks and *on-time performance reviews*. Employees want feedback on how they are doing and should receive it daily on an informal basis and formally on a regular basis. The performance review should be taken very seriously and supervisors should be rated as to how well and how thoroughly they perform this very important task. Most facilities supervisors don't do well on this and training is essential on this subject.

Isn't it interesting that in many companies, wages and salaries comprise 50-70% of their revenue base and yet budget less than 1% for training? Training not only pays for itself but generally provides a minimum return on investment of 30:1. Not training people just doesn't make sense. Even if training isn't in your budget, do it because the cost will usually be covered through savings or productivity improvements within the same budget year. And, training provides other benefits in that employees seldom quit while they are being trained and morale increases. And remember Zig Ziglar's quote, *"The only thing worse than training your employees and losing them, is not training them and keeping them."*

WITHOUT FORGETTING TO BE EFFICIENT AND EFFECTIVE

Finally, we should be thinking about our other customer—management—who expects us to be efficient and effective. Their goals always include satisfying the stockholders who invest in the company with the expectation of getting a good return on their investment. **Facilities management is not an overhead cost, but a contributor to the bottom line that provides cost effective and efficient services which enhance the assets managed and provides services required by their internal customers.**

Our focus should be not on how much we spend but on how much we save and how efficient and productive we are. Again, the key attribute that management focuses on is the profit and loss statement (P&L). Strongly encourage all managers to review the P&L with the entire staff in order to inform them of the financial health of the company as well as to solicit ideas on what went right that month and what areas of improvement still exist. A lot of great ideas can be generated in this manner.

Doing the above will build customer loyalty and employees will become enthusiastic about their jobs and proud to work in the department. Feedback from both will make top management take notice and recognize the contributions made by facilities management. The importance of leaving customers with positive perceptions become the foundation for your future success. And, when the team wins, individuals get recognized and promoted in the organizations.

9

THE VALUE OF FACILITIES MANAGEMENT

Facilities managers are not doing an effective job of measuring and communicating the value of the services they provide to their companies. Maintenance budgets have declined more than 30 percent in real terms, bringing the deferred maintenance backlog to new highs. Current budgets are inadequate and provide only one-half of the funding needed to preserve building stock. By the year 2000, our nation's public infrastructure will amount to more than $1.0 trillion in deferred maintenance due to lack of resources currently budgeted. A related problem is that there still is a large amount of energy being wasted by these poorly maintained, inefficient buildings.

Facilities managers typically complain that maintenance is the first area affected by budget cuts or is underbudgeted initially. Too often, the maintenance budget is treated as a reserve fund, supplying a capital for what are deemed the most important needs. The facilities manager has to be aggressive to get his/her points across to top management. Outside pressures routinely competing with maintenance needs include federally or state-mandated programs involving asbestos abatement, recycling, compliance with the

Americans with Disabilities Act (ADA), ozone reduction and pe-troleum tank removal programs, all of which carry no funds of their own. Other similar mandates are funded from maintenance budgets; often, small capital projects amounting to a third or more of the maintenance budget are incorrectly reported as maintenance.

Administrators of building programs must become better sales people and be able to make presentations that are stated in terms that top management can understand. Often the key factor in a company's decision to undertake a major facilities management in-vestment is the credibility and past track record of the person mak-ing the proposal, since many of the benefits of facilities manage-ment are simply not quantifiable.

Too many facilities managers are not capable of overcoming administrative barriers, such as lack of administrative focus on fa-cilities problem areas, lack of understanding of the cost of owner-ship, lack of concern for building management, and organizational culture. In order to make a dent on the growing problem of de-ferred maintenance, high level meetings must occur to discuss the issues and to foster trust between facilities managers and top man-agement. A champion is needed for the program.

MEASURING THE COSTS AND BENEFITS

Once top management recognizes that their assets are effectively managed, they will re-prioritize their leadership agenda. That is easier said than done, because it is difficult to measure accurately the costs and benefits of facilities management. Peter Drucker has often been quoted: "If you can't measure it, you can't manage it." And Lord Kelvin stated: "Without measurement we have only art, not science."

Prior to communicating with top management, we should be able to answer these questions: How well is facilities management doing and how do we know how well facilities management is do-ing (i.e., the measurement issue)? It is important to understand that companies will be decentralizing and calling upon all functions not only to be more efficient but also to provide a "sustainable competitive advantage" to the overall enterprise. So, one of our measuring sticks should be to determine how top management tracks maintenance to satisfy themselves that facilities management is doing a good job.

There is no simple answer to this apparently simple question. The answer is at least three-dimensional. A distinction should be made between the management of facilities management and the facilities management function. How well is the facilities management "business" being run? Here, technical measures such as response times, uptime, etc. are appropriate and financial measures, such as budget compliance, and managerial measures, such as employee turnover and schedule, can be used effectively.

The time dimension also comes into play. Are current operations being successfully managed in a cost effective, timely manner? Many operational measures are available to track these variables. On the other hand, is future development being managed and directed effectively? Measures of schedule and budget performance are important as well as system quality and functionality.

The external focus is even more important. What is facilities management doing to contribute to the success of the organization? As the scope moves to an enterprise-wide orientation, the measures become more difficult to quantify. Bottom-line contributions, cost savings and cost avoidance are easily understood by top management, and the facilities manager should look for these before any others.

Other ways of measuring the enterprise-wide contributions of facilities management include the following issues: Is the benefit one of increased efficiency and productivity? Does it improve the organizational and managerial effectiveness? Or is it of sufficient strategic and competitive impact that it can transform the business? Can it become a product or service in its own right? Here, business measures and judgment must be applied however imprecise they may be. Steering committees, task forces, user surveys and charging schemes are a few of the subjective assessment approaches that may be used.

FACILITIES MANAGEMENT BENCHMARKS

Significant progress has been made in recent years in an effort to arrive at benchmarks that can be used universally to quantify the results of effective facilities management. Benchmarks include:

- Training to keep technicians current should be allocated at $1,000 per FTE annually for simple HVAC systems to more than $4,000 per FTE for complex systems [Swanson, 1991].
- Increasing energy savings to cover 100 percent of the personnel costs of maintenance over a two-year period [Minden, 1991].
- Developing a national standard of 5.3 percent of total budget to be allocated for maintenance [Smith, 1988].
- Developing national budgets of 2 percent annually of the replacement value of the building(s) and 0.5 to 1.5 percent more annually if the building does not meet current codes [Dunn, 1989].
- If large amounts of deferred maintenance exist, these percentages should be increased over time to cover extra costs of correcting this problem.
- A 12-year simple payback or less may be viewed as a good way of measuring use of scarce resources.
- Use of multi-trade preventive maintenance management (PMM) crews to rotate through buildings has been effective. Good PMM can keep 60 percent of building equipment and systems from failing [Dillow, 1989].
- Heat pump PMM will save 50 percent of the cost of corrective or breakdown maintenance [Syska & Hennesey, 1983].
- PMM can increase the manufacturer's predicted life of equipment by 50 percent or more [Shear, 1983].
- Maintenance training of staff should be planned for, and on complex training, vendors should retrain at six months and 18 months to make sure operators have retained knowledge [Swanson, 1981].

- Commissioning new buildings has shown a 2-to-1 benefits-to-cost ratio [Trueman, 1989]. Commissioning involves using experts to complete a dynamic point-by-point evaluation of a facility against design specifications.
- Designing for maintainability provides the best, sure answer to cost avoidance in the future [Damiani,1983].

10

WHY CONSIDER OUTSOURCING?

Is It Viable?

Ever since Peter Drucker was quoted in a *Wall Street Journal* article in 1990 saying that American companies should "sell their mailroom" (i.e., outsource everything that does not give your company a competitive edge), I have been an adversary of outsourcing. I have been in facilities management ever since I was a "co-op" at Drexel University. My first jobs were in maintenance engineering and maintenance has become my special interest, although I have been responsible for the full spectrum of facilities management as an owner's representative for most of my career. I've written articles on effective maintenance management, spoken at educational conferences and trained maintenance personnel. Along the way, I've acquired both knowledge and bias.

Many companies followed Drucker's advice. In fact, most companies today use business gauges such as profit per employee to measure performance. Is it any wonder why downsizing in maintenance has occurred? This has led to trimming facilities management departments in favor of contracted services. Although other departments have been affected, none has been hit as hard as facilities management. In many companies, it has become part of a facility manager's job to evaluate outsourcing as a viable alternative. This has led to outsourcing many facilities services such as janitorial, security, mail/courier, landscaping/grounds, energy management, property management and food services.

Most facilities managers have held on tightly to mechanical/electrical maintenance services because they felt strongly that in-house services were better and they could not receive true value in the "contracting out" process. I share that opinion but I have learned that, if properly done, outsourcing is a viable alternative that can save you money without sacrificing quality. In fact, quality of service can increase if the right contractor is selected and if the selection process is built on a philosophy of a long-term relationship.

Are these following "in-house" HVAC employee problems familiar to you?

- Tardiness/sick leave abuse
- Negative attitudes
- Not properly performing rounds. Is equipment inspected and operating readings of this equipment taken by each shift?
- Engineers not communicating with security and office staff. Engineers are required to stay in communication with the security staff after office staff departs for the day. When working in noisy or inaccessible areas such as roof, attic, rotary compressor room or any areas where radios or beepers are known to be a problem, are whereabouts reported to security or office staff? Does your dispatcher know the location of employees at all times?
- Leaving premises without permission during regular or overtime shifts
- Failure to perform work assignments
- Failure to report critical equipment problems

- Failure to repair critical equipment in a timely manner or the first time
- Poor repair and maintenance techniques
- Poor housekeeping practices in shop and equipment areas
- Failure to clean up work after completing assignments
- Lack of concentrated effort to get to work during emergency situations
- Failure to plan work arrival in anticipation of weather problems
- Failure to pass on work assignments to shift relief personnel or to leave adequate instructions for continuation of work assignments
- Failure to order and track parts properly
- Poor image
- Low productivity
- Poorly trained
- Refusal to change in a changing world
- Standing around, socializing

Managing the maintenance operation has never been easy and the above problems have been around for decades. *One thing for certain is that if they don't change and change quickly, outsourcing surely will result.*

CONSTRUCTIVE AND DESTRUCTIVE OUTSOURCING

Facilities Design and Management magazine offers a newsletter called "The Outsource Report" which they say will serve as a primer, planning tool and guide to the facilities manager and top management as they explore their options concerning outsourcing. Their advertising suggests that outsourcing is inevitable and it is better to be "ahead of the curve" and become a corporate hero by making the right choice, to save "dollars."

I am in agreement with their contention that outsourcing is the single most compelling business issue facing our profession. I am also in agreement with them that outsourcing will be increasing at a faster rate as we enter the 21st century. In fact the market may even hit the $30B mark by the year 2003 (three times as much outsourcing than today's figures). However, I also believe that outsourcing should be evaluated closely before making a decision to save "short term" dollars.

Outsourcing reminds me of the downsizing which prevailed in the 1990s. A recent study in *Business Week* (4/28/97) concluded that:

- downsizing has had little if any positive impact on company earnings or stock performance;
- companies now face serious morale problems due to years of restructuring;
- disability/stress claims are higher in organizations who downsized;
- displaced managers bringing wrongful termination suits are winning their law suits half the time.

I haven't read many true success stories about companies who outsourced and I believe that I know why. There aren't many success stories to tell. Also, the surviving employees are scared and have no company loyalty. I'm not saying that outsourcing won't work because in many cases, it is a viable alternative, especially when the selection process is well thought out and applied properly. A facilities manager should be proactive and always look at outsourcing as an option. At the same time he/she should be mindful that the road to true success in outsourcing is not only saving money but also in building business friendships with the outsourcer and that starts with building friendships with company employees, who are affected in the process.

I say friendships rather than partnerships because many partnerships, like marriages, end in divorce. I've talked to several heads of maintenance who have indicated that they've had problems in finding contractors who are committed to handling their service needs and in doing a quality job. The problem is that almost all contractors start off with great promises and a great appreciation for the work. After a few months, their zeal and interest diminishes. A full commitment has to come from both sides and yet, the goals of doing a quality job and maximizing profit contradict each other. Guess which one wins out. Outsourcers are generally intrepreneurs who no one gave a chance to succeed while on the inside. So they went outside to make money for themselves instead of for the company and its stockholders.

True friendships need to happen for a long, trusting relationship to evolve. Too many contractors don't recognize the true value of each individual employee. For example, in outsourcing, contractors make money by reducing staff, especially middle management. I've heard stories of 170 people being fired in the morning and later in the same afternoon, 130 of those fired being rehired. The memories of that action will live forever in the minds and hearts of the affected employees, including the survivors. Do you believe that these employees will ever be motivated to do their best or do you believe that they will only do what's necessary? The heart of productivity is *people*.

Facilities management is indeed a major target of outsourcing. That is a fact. In the plant, facilities management, and especially maintenance is a core business, but even in that scenario, facilities management is a target. Why? Because we haven't educated top management otherwise. We can take lots of positive steps to educate and sell management on the many contributions we make to the bottom line. We can become more efficient and effective and persuade management toward that end. Once convinced, do you believe that management would rid themselves of a department that is efficient, effective and contributes to the bottom line? I don't think so.

Our major problem is leadership and we need to develop more leaders in facilities management. Obtain these skills and welcome the opportunity to examine outsourcing as an alternative that may be helpful in accomplishing your company's and your department's goals and objectives. As former U.S. Senator Everett Dirkson says,

"When I feel the heat, I see the light." The heat is here and it's time we see the light. Be involved in the process or someone else will.

MANAGING OUTSOURCING

Let's take a closer look at the outsourcing process and see what you can do to make it work. One definition of outsourcing is the subcontracting of services by a corporation or institution in order to compete more effectively and deliver product/services with the greatest possible value. I can understand how outsourcing saves money on a short term basis but do not understand where *value* comes into play. Reducing numbers of people in the manner it usually works is not productive in the long run because it reduces intrinsic knowledge. It should take the form of complementing and supplementing in-house efforts.

Today's corporations are now beginning to mend the fences that need repair as a result of radical downsizing that occurred in the 1990s. Watson Wyatt, a well recognized human resources consulting firm is actively marketing their new people management programs using an advertisement, "Now that you've taken your company apart, how do you put the people back together?" Restructuring and downsizing may have changed some companies for the better but it may have weakened something vital to their competitive edge—the commitment of your people. People are the only thing you have that your competition doesn't and people must be involved in the process, if productivity gains can be reasonably expected. It's amazing what people will do if they are treated well, respected, involved and work in a positive caring environment. If the goal is to gain a competitive edge, invest in people.

In fact, progressive companies are trying to build more leaders from within by focusing on management behavior. Learn to tap the creative and productive potential of the workforce. I can't imagine how outsourcing can achieve these goals without focusing on building up their staff instead of tearing it apart.

By judiciously supplementing its in-house workforce with adaptive out-tasking, a facility management/maintenance department can meet and exceed the advantages of outsourcing. Top management wants to see more productivity, cost savings and a better image in facilities and we can provide this *if* we do the following, which will make us indispensable, and unstoppable.

A STEPWISE PATH TO SUCCESS IN MANAGEMENT

Facilities management seldom receives top management's attention, unless of course something goes wrong. And who wants that kind of recognition? Positive attention and proper recognition can best be achieved by demonstrating "bottom-line" contributions, and success will come to those who effectively communicate the impact to his/her superiors through demonstrated proficiency.

Success can be achieved in a number of ways. The following suggestions will go a long way in helping you get the attention you deserve from top management:

1. *Know the business of business.* This is easier said than done, however, it is essential. Your department's contributions should be measured against the company's goals and objectives and other strategic planning initiatives. Facilities departments should be prepared to endure both progress and back sliding when either is in the company's best interests. There is an increasing emphasis on management rather than technical competence, and the facilities manager must keep up with the state-of-the-art technology and be flexible enough to turn on a dime with programs that are keeping with the company's strategic plans.

2. *Improve the image and efficiency of maintenance other support services.* Take a hard look at the department and stop accepting mediocrity. Maintenance is generally viewed as the most non-productive department in a plant, with minimal standards and quality, ineffective labor, scheduling and some maintenance techniques dating back 100 years. Part of a manager's job is to study outsourcing as an alternative to onboard facilities man-

agement. Take an objective look into all aspects of maintenance to see if positive results can be obtained through outsourcing. Perhaps outsourcing is a better answer. If you aren't
concerned and proactive in this area, someone else in top management will do the job for you. Good maintenance equates to
increased capacity of the plant.

3. *Educate your boss/don't sell him.* As stated earlier, management is usually ignorant (meaning uninformed) regarding the
positive contributions made by facilities managers. We all believe that the boss knows a lot about what we do. He doesn't
and can't, unless we tell him, and it is not only proper but also
essential that we do communicate. Remember, communication
should be in terms that top management can understand—and
shouldn't be done in a self-serving manner. It is important for
top management to know the positive side of facilities management, especially as it affects the bottom line. Use logic and
know when to listen.

4. *Document your savings, cost containment, costs avoidance,
productivity increases/Know difference between ROI and
structured risk.* Every time you make or save money, report it.
Compile reports on a weekly, monthly, quarterly and yearly basis and ensure that they get into the right hands. You'll be surprised at year end of your accomplishments.

5. *Think "bottom-line."* In most cases every dollar saved in overhead is a dollar added to the bottom line. Some managers
spend every penny they receive in approved budgets because
they feel that they will receive less the following year. This is a
sure way to fail. Zero-based budgeting, by line item, should be
a standard practice with a hard comparative look taken at the
costs of outsourcing alternatives, which in some cases can be
less expensive and more efficient than in-house solutions.

6. *Look for opportunities to make money or reduce costs.* You
can be an outsourcing alternative to someone else. There are
many documented cases where one company is performing
services for another or two companies have combined resources
to keep O/M costs at a minimum. Try something new and

creative, get rid of what you don't do well, and get better at what you do well.

7. *Write articles and speak to groups.* Share your expertise and experience. Most companies are highly supportive of outside involvement of employees and publicize these activities in their company newsletters. That's one way of communicating to, and gaining the attention of, top management. Also, the experience you gain in writing and speaking is valuable training; one which will help you sell ideas inside your organization. And you will always learn from the audience.

8. *Participate in professional societies/community organizations.* Most companies are good corporate citizens in that they give back to the community they serve. Companies take pride in those employees who serve their community. Become active in professional societies, company sponsored functions, community service and in the political process and you will be recognized in a positive manner. Teaching in-house seminars as well as outside the company in your area of expertise also will be widely recognized. You will be provided opportunities for leadership positions and be honored for your accomplishments.

9. *Take the initiative and speak up.* Be proactive and make your views known early in a positive, constructive manner. Accept and positively respond to criticism rather than being negative and defensive about it. Learn to say "no" tactfully to requestors of service who make impossible or unrealistic demands and better yet, look for ways to say "yes" and work cooperatively with others. And don't be a complainer—solve the problem, don't be a part of it.

10. *Motivate others.* Learn to lead and be a leader, a manager of others. Lead by example: work early, stay late, make decisions expeditiously, give credit to others, and answer phone calls promptly. These are examples of good work habits which others should follow. Let people know that you respect others who get the job done, no matter how busy they are.

11. *Plan, plan, plan.* Plan your department's work and your work to be in step with your company's plans. Plan ahead and follow-up. Proper planning is the key to accomplishment.

12. *Understand financial statements.* Those who can fully understand financial statements seem to progress much faster in their careers. It is important to express your plans in a manner that presents financial impacts of various alternatives and can evaluate the alternatives in an objective manner. Financial expertise is of growing strategic importance in today's increasingly challenging and competitive environment. Spend time with the accounting department and work with them. Facilities management is a financially based function. The likelihood of outsourcing would be limited if we understood finance a bit more than we do.

13. *Train, train, train.* Keep others trained as well as yourself. The importance of training can't be overemphasized, especially training that is tied into organizational goals. Specific training that focuses on converting weaknesses to strengths is generally most helpful and yields the most results from training monies available. Remember, few people quit while in training. As Zig Ziglar says, "The only thing worse than training your employees and losing them, is not training them and keeping them.

14. *Be a "changemaster"* View change that is made for competitive reasons as an opportunity that will yield better results. Most people resist change and must be educated as to the value of the change that is occurring. Today, and in the future, change will be a way of working life and rapid adjustment and adaptability to change is essential. Leaders lead change and lead by example. Jack Welch says, "If the rate of change inside a company is less than the rate of change outside, the end is in sight." A new level of facilities manager has emerged over the last decade, one who has come out of the backroom and takes on responsibilities other than pure facilities under their wings. Today's facilities manager must be administratively trained and adaptable to any condition that affects his/her company. They should be leaders who are capable of managing all services and show no fear of change. In fact, they should relish change and the opportunities that change brings.

Today's facilities managers must be able to communicate effectively on all levels. They must be strong and well respected by their peers, as well as top management. They must listen and give credit where credit is due. They must be planners and organizers who "follow up" well and care for their company, their profession and their fellow employees, in that order. And they must be "champions" of outsourcing i.e. they study and evaluate its potential contributions before the CEO/CFO get involved.

Companies who haven't outsourced genuinely are concerned with security measures, loss of management control and possible deterioration of quality—all of which are legitimate reasons to pay more and stay in-house. Their major concern regarding quality is that contractors will do as little as possible in order to increase profits. In short, they want to obtain high quality maintenance for their dollars; in other words, *value*. The question is: are there contractors in your area that can deliver *value*, measure it and communicate it properly to management? If so invite them in to talk about how they could augment your workforce in order to become more efficient and effective. In a nutshell, it's difficult to make sweeping generalities about what's better. Remember quality and value are never gained by understaffing a job.

Great companies never profit at the expense of their employees. They care for their employees and invest in them. Study outsourcing. Work with outsourcers. But, be careful before making a hasty decision. Good luck.

QUALIFICATION PROCESS

The recipe for success in outsourcing is in qualifying suppliers and writing good requests for proposals (RFPs). The following is recommended as a process to use for qualifying contractors.

Evaluate the Company

- Is it a local company?
- Years in business?

- Turnover rate?
- Financial stability?
- Quality of training program?
- Does contractor provide quality training?
- Quality of management staff?
- Technical expertise?
- Understanding of CMMS, EMS, IAQ, etc.?
- Similar experience?
- Number of buildings operated?
- Square feet of buildings operated?
- Specific HVAC system(s) experience?
- Number of licensed technicians?
- Compatibility?
- Adaptability?
- Quality of apprentice program?

Evaluate the Personnel

- How long has the management team been in place?
- Interview the engineer/project manager who will be assigned to the job
- Ensure longevity of the engineer for your project
- Review resumes carefully

Visit Office and Several Job Sites

- Interview current customers
- Review entire organization
- Ask for a list of references of similar projects from the contractor and a list of jobs that they have lost in the last five years (and the reason why)
- Review their operations (how interface and communication will occur between customer and supplier)

Convey Your Expectations Clearly

- Transition plan
- Performance standards (response time, meetings, quality standards, reports, etc.)
- Dress code
- Licensing requirements

Request multi-year pricing. The base contract should be for three years, with at least two one-year options.

Identify Pricing Format/Agreement

- Insurance requirements
- Fixed price
- Time and materials

Request that suppliers visit your site and perform a facilities audit of mechanical systems indicating the strengths and weaknesses they see in your current operation. Have them also indicate whether or not they are willing to interview your existing employees and place them on their payroll.

EVALUATE PROPOSALS

The low bid is not always the best bid. Interview and select the most qualified suppliers, and negotiate reasonable rates.

Outsourcing has filled the gap created by downsizing and lack of training of in-house maintenance workers, and in many cases has been responsive to the needs of productive maintenance work forces. Owners/facility managers should investigate outsourcing as a viable alternative to obtain the results they desire. Again, the process must be done properly and qualified contractors can alleviate your concerns. Outsourcing may just be the right thing for you. A *qualified* contractor, however, will also let you know if outsourcing is not best for you. If you pick the right contractor, you won't need to be concerned about supervising them. They will be an asset instead of a liability. Look at outsourcing as a long-term partnership—one which will continuously improve over time. If you believe that the best qualified contractor can measure up to this performance standard and add value to your operation, then go with it.

11

MAXIMIZING INDOOR AIR QUALITY

Several years ago, I was in the U.S. Postmaster General's Office for a meeting and couldn't help but notice a mobile that hung directly over the table where we were seated. The mobile was made up of "pointing fingers," which constantly moved and pointed at each conferee. It reminded me of my profession, facilities management. *A facilities manager is responsible for planning, designing, building, operating and maintaining buildings.* Each direct report for each of these functions usually blames the other, or their consultants and contractors, for any problem that crops ups. In many organizations these functions are split among departments, which makes criticism even more pronounced.

Finger-pointing and blaming others is easy but certainly doesn't get anything constructively done. Designers don't design right, builders don't build right and the operations and maintenance staff don't operate or maintain the facility properly. For 35 years, I've heard reasons why things can't be done and it's becoming even more prevalent in the industry when discussing indoor air quality

(IAQ). In the absence of regulations, there is no incentive in the industry to pursue IAQ. Building owners deny that problems exist until a lawsuit is filed or building tenants threaten to leave. Once that occurs, everyone become defensive. It's too late at that point.

The fact of the matter is that there is a little bit of truth in all allegations:

- Design professionals do not design for maintainability and operational efficiency; initial cost is usually the primary criteria and consequently, HVAC systems become a victim of cost cutting through value engineering.
- Facilities maintenance has been both downsized and outsourced since 1990, making the function less efficient and effective.
- Funds for training have virtually been nonexistent or reduced dramatically. But this still does not lessen the facility manager's responsibility of providing good IAQ.

GROWING DECREASE IN RESOURCES

In the last three years I have observed a growing decrease in overall maintenance resources. Many building owners have even resorted to "run-to-fail" maintenance strategies. For the last ten years, I've also observed a growing increase in deferred maintenance. Owners are not replacing system and sub-system equipment when they should. Deferred maintenance is at an all-time high and a real problem in America. All of this has had a real effect on IAQ and it is a problem that has to be solved now. The financial consequences are too great to continue ignoring it and look the other way. Tenants and other building occupants are demanding health and comfort conditions and are suing to make their point. It's sad to see this occur because **80% of the problems can be handled cost effectively through good maintenance,** which just isn't happening. The cost of absenteeism and loss of productivity and morale alone greatly outweigh the cost to properly operate and maintain the facility, including the long overdue replacement of mechanical systems, subsystems and equipment.

Improper or inadequate maintenance is the real culprit of poor IAQ, not inadequate ventilation, which is often depicted as representing 52 percent of all IAQ problems. A close look would reveal problems with air distribution and balancing, poor HVAC maintenance, temperature, humidity and filtration concerns. And, who is to say that bringing in more outside air is good. Tell that to allergy sufferers or facilities managers who have to maintain positive pressurization in their facilities in order to keep dirt and pollution out. Also, some locales are just plain dirty, especially near our airports, tunnels, cities, and highways.

I was in a facility recently that had an excellent HVAC system which included humidity controls and building automation. During a walk through, we found one stage of the two-stage 175-ton chiller was not operating. The energy management system and humidifier were turned off; three of seven energy-efficient hot water heaters were off line; the cooling tower was not being maintained, and it had missing insulation and heat tape for winter operation; and mechanical rooms were both filthy and disorderly, used as stock rooms and storage areas. Does this sound familiar? The entire building was being operated manually and the chief engineer blamed everything on maintenance cost cuts. Many older buildings have similar problems.

Other common problems found in buildings over five years of age are that 20-25 percent of VAV boxes are not operative because of inattention and poor maintenance, economizers aren't being maintained, and HVAC system components such as air handlers and ductwork are dirty and operating well out of tolerance. When a system is out of tolerance, nuisance calls such as hot spots, cold spots and "bad air" calls increase. In many cases, it is possible to correct the situation at a cost significantly less than the annual repairs and additional energy cost that had been spent to date. It usually makes financial sense to maintain equipment properly; however, many companies don't know how to plan, schedule, track and measure maintenance in a meaningful way and many do not educate their management on the importance of excellence in maintenance.

OUTCOMES OF POOR MAINTENANCE

What are tenants and building occupants doing about poor IAQ? On an increasing basis, they are banding together in proactive task groups and demanding to see test results for lead in water, legionella in cooling towers and domestic water systems, recent balancing reports, maintenance logs on variable air volume (VAV) boxes and flex duct, CO_2 in indoor air, and requesting regular tours of mechanical rooms and penthouses to ensure that the equipment and areas are kept whistle clean. Tenants and building occupants are meeting as representative groups regularly (usually monthly) and invite the facilities manager/maintenance manager to their meetings. If their problems are not addressed promptly, they often call the U.S. Public Health Service to complain and ask them to perform testing and become involved.

Litigation is becoming a daily fact of life. The number of IAQ cases has been rising substantially and the damages sought is alarming. We generally don't hear about them because most are settled out of court. Legal expenses and financial settlements have been very high and when this is combined with loss of productivity, it would seem prudent for building owners to be proactive and invest the relatively small amount needed to operate and maintain a building properly. It's just not happening. Because of the huge risk involved with IAQ, most insurance companies have incorporated "pollution exclusion" clauses in their policies.

IAQ MAINTENANCE IS AN OBLIGATION

I believe that you, as a facilities manager and the person responsible for IAQ in your building, have the obligation to inform and educate senior management as to the risks involved with reduced maintenance, and to develop a comprehensive operating and maintenance (O&M) program to minimize the risk. Following are a few suggestions for facilities managers who are proposing IAQ strategies to their management.

Improve the Image and Efficiency
of Maintenance

CMMS and EMS can be combined on one PC-based computer at reasonable costs. You can also incorporate and monitor CO^2 and air flow sensors as part of the combined system. This can help you document maintenance and manage IAQ.

Use Videos to Illustrate/Justify Your Needs

Video-taping problem areas will do more to justify the need to repair/replace equipment than anything else you can do. Using videos after repairs are done will help you educate management and employee groups on why excellence in maintenance is both necessary and cost-effective in your organization. Videos also are great in establishing a library and documentation for your facility. They will not only let you tell the story but also show the ending.

Think Productivity

Ask yourself, before doing anything, if what you are thinking of doing will affect or impact employee productivity. This particularly applies to renovation work, roof repairs, painting, HVAC repairs, and plumbing repairs. How will the implementation affect overall productivity? Although we all hate paying additional premiums for "after-hours" or weekend work, it may be the least expensive way to get these jobs done. Also, it is wise to involve the building occupants who will be affected by the work and to keep them informed.

Review IAQ Management Measures
During Construction

Often IAQ problems occur in new buildings that are turned over to maintenance too quickly. Improper installation of HVAC equipment and misapplied temperature control strategies are all too common and are the result of improper commissioning, too-quick turnovers and insufficient training for operating personnel. Allowing adequate shakedown for temperature control systems is also important in turning over new buildings.

Maintain Your Economizer

Improperly working economizers directly contribute to complaints of inadequate ventilation, often resulting in overheating of the building and negative building pressure, which leads to excessive infiltration. Very seldom will you see well maintained economizers in buildings.

Develop an IAQ Response Team

Many IAQ complaints can be resolved quickly by a competent, sensitive, caring O&M staff who will respond quickly to all complaints, take all complaints seriously and provide feedback as soon as practical. Training in attitude and interpersonal skills and constant communication until a solution is reached is a must. Prompt and professional response to IAQ complaints will resolve a majority of cases.

Communicate with Building Occupants

Establish IAQ news bulletin boards and locate them in prominent locations such as elevator lobbies, coffee break areas or cafeterias. Proactively post news of interest on IAQ facility bulletins posting scheduling and explaining work going on, and offer tours of mechanical rooms/penthouses and customer service areas to demonstrate capabilities of your CMMS/EMS. Include information and forms used for employees to register complaints. Feedback on resolution of complaints should also be shared with building occupants.

Establish Proactive Legionella Preventive Maintenance Measures

This should include simple measures such as heat and flush, which is an inexpensive way to control legionella in domestic water systems on a regular basis. Hot water temperatures are raised to 160°F and faucets/shower heads are flushed for 30 minutes. This procedure can be repeated two to three times over several days until no legionella is recovered from the taps.

The above recommendations should go a long way toward solving most IAQ problems and are cost-effective, basic measures that should be a standard for all buildings.

DID YOU KNOW?

- Clean coils improve IAQ; enhance operational efficiency; increase life of motors, compressors and bearings; and has a payback (through utilities savings) of less than 1 year.

- Improving operational efficiency of HVAC systems/subsystems obtained through a good maintenance program pays for itself in less than 6 months. Plus, it minimizes nuisance calls, allowing maintenance personnel to be more productive.

12

QUALITY IS
AN ATTITUDE

During the past five years our profession has been decimated by downsizing, deferred maintenance, outsourcing and loss of resources. It has gotten to a point where the process seems nearly irreversible. Since 1990, maintenance has taken the brunt of early retirements and downsizing [made in the good name of total quality management/continuous quality improvement (TQM/CQI)] and we have lost many of our leaders and role models in the process. Deferred maintenance is at an all-time high and lack of resources allocated to maintenance has been on a downward spiral, resulting in less training for existing staff. Furthermore, fewer young workers are entering the maintenance field, making outsourcing inevitable in the future. And this trend doesn't appear as if it will get any better as I look forward into the next millennium. This disturbing trend in our profession will cause us to get down on ourselves and our profession, but that's a loser's attitude. We've got to think and act like the winners we are.

A WINNING ATTITUDE

I believe that it is how people feel about themselves that helps drive productivity. People who feel good about themselves produce good results. Can we make or help make people feel good about themselves? Can we touch the lives of people who work with us? Can we make a difference? We can and here's how.

Let's stop whining and start winning. As leaders in the facilities management profession, our job is to individually and collectively create a positive, caring environment and teach employees - despite the obstacles–to develop a positive attitude and be positively motivated. Dedicated, motivated employees working in a positive, caring environment can produce up to 100 percent more (according to James Burke, former chairman of Johnson & Johnson). We've been lulled to sleep by our environment and have been conditioned over the past five years to believe that we are helpless and cannot change our plight. That is wrong! Let's wake up and be proactive in providing solutions to our dilemma and not be part of the problem. No one is going to do it for us.

A recent study disclosed that there was no direct correlation found between high school valedictorians and success. Does that surprise you? If attitude was taught in the home and school and the same results were found, would that be surprising? It would to me. In Japan, one hour of every school day (ages 3-18) is spent on developing good attitudes and in the home, children are encouraged to be the best that they can be. Is it any wonder why Japan has become a very successful nation?

Everyone wants to be successful, however, few people truly become successful. Look around you and name people and organizations that you consider successful and you will find that they *all* have positive attitudes. Listen carefully to those who succeed as they credit attitude, not aptitude, as the significant difference behind their success. We live in a negative world. By the time a person reaches 18 years old he/she will have heard the word "no" over 148,000 times. People get in life what they expect. The problem is that 90% of us expect to do poorly and we must raise the level of our expectations of ourselves and others in order to be successful.

100

Many people feel that the opposite of success is failure. It is conformance and accepting mediocrity. Failure is the foundation for success. It is an event, not a person. Having and maintaining a positive attitude is important to success. It is the result of new thinking-believing in yourself, focusing on successes, learning from failure and surrounding yourself with people who share your values, principles, and thinking.

Success = ATTITUDE + SKILLS + KNOWLEDGE. Success is not measured against others. It is how you compare based on what you could have done with what you have got. Success is saying, "today I'm going to give it my best shot" and knowing at the end of the day that you have done your best.

IMPLEMENTING THE PROGRAM

"Doing more with less" will continue to be a common goal of facility departments in the twenty-first century since companies will want to continue to expand without adding additional employees. How can you go about implementing a program that will yield the results you want to achieve–improved image, efficiency and productivity–while containing/reducing costs, which in the service business is our bottom line?

Between 1991–1994, I had an opportunity to work for the Montgomery County, Maryland government, heading their Facilities and Services Department and leading the county's initiatives in quality. During that time I instituted what I named a golden attitude program in the department, which produced amazing results in quality, delivery of service and reduced costs/enhanced revenues. In fact the results were so good and the program was so well accepted throughout the county, I wrote my first book, *Looking for the Gold* on the process I used. I'm happy to share some of this experience with you in the following pages.

Phase I

The seeds for the Department of Facilities and Services (DFS) Golden Attitude program in Montgomery County, Maryland were planted in August 1991 and the program formally began in January 1992. In that time period, educational workshops (2-1/2 hours long) on attitude were presented to all employees in groups of 50. The book, *Building a Positive Attitude in Yourself and Others,* by Rich Wilkins, was given to every employee as supplemental reading. The workshops were designed to raise awareness as to the importance of attitude to team building and individual success in the work place, as well as in the family, which impacts the work place.

Nearly six months was allocated for the introductory preparation phase in consideration that it takes time to develop trust between employees and all levels of management and for employees to accept the idea as worthwhile. Unless the program was "bought in" by everyone, it would not be successful.

In addition, face-to-face meetings with individuals and employee groups were used to reinforce the workshops. Excellence workshops, made up of representatives of all employee groups and customer groups, were and are still being held for the express purpose of obtaining feedback and continually modifying the overall program. A vision statement and new mission statement for the department was developed through a similar workshop and some common mottoes and names for the program came out of "listening down" and involving employees.

DFS MISSION:
Meeting Customer's Challenges with Innovative Solutions

GOLDEN ATTITUDE PROGRAM:
1. DFS ..... where attitude *is* the difference
2. Looking for the *gold*

MOTTOS:
1. DFS ..... where you can expect the exceptional

2. DFS ..... a *team* of service-oriented people dedicated to providing extraordinary service with a commitment for quality and *caring*.

3. C^2S
   - Customer
   - County
   - Self

These soon caught on with most employee groups. With the involvement of our employees, I recognized that we were on the right track with the program and my major role changed to serving as a teacher/coach/cheerleader, encouraging ever more participation by everyone during the process and satisfying their thirst for more knowledge and training.

Phase 2

In Rich Wilkins' book, he mentioned Zig Ziglar on many occasions and indicated that he was a student of Zig Ziglar. I learned who Zig Ziglar was and sent for a catalogue of his materials. I also learned of his *See You at the Top* book and seminars, which were available on video tape and audio cassette. The video program consisted of 12 videos and accompanying materials. The videos were 35-40 minutes each and educational and entertaining in nature. The tapes focused on the topics of "Foundation for Success," "Building Positive Attitudes," "Raising Self Esteem and Self Confidence," "Setting and Achieving Goals," "Hard Work and Desire."

Within the same time period, we experimented by offering Ziglar videos (sometimes up to three times a day in order to accommodate all shifts) to employees who were interested in seeing them. Minimal work time was taken in the process, since employees used their lunch time to view the videos. No one was forced to attend. It became an event that was not only well accepted but also became enormously successful. Some employees saw the videos up to five times.

We decided to augment the Ziglar *See You at the Top* program with other individual video cassettes by Rich Wilkins, Brian Tracy and Les Brown, and a variety of audio cassettes that employees could borrow and bring home. At least twenty employees requested the videos to take home for their families in the first two months. We not only accommodated that practice but also encouraged it. Ziglar videos are still being seen at the DFS Theater and being borrowed on a routine basis by employees and outside corporations who heard about what we were doing and inquired about the program.

Phase 3

In January 1992, the employee recognition program, based on Golden Attitude criteria, formally began and has been continuing without a hitch. In the first year of the program more than 110 employees were recognized by their management for *extraordinary* contributions. Here's how it worked:

Employees were nominated each month by management within their divisions and the division chief orally presented the candidates to his/her peers indicating examples of the employee's specific contributions. Those employees who received *unanimous* approval by upper management received a Golden Attitude pin, a framed certificate, attitude poster, attitude of gratitude balloon, and wide recognition in *Par Excellence* (the departmental newsletter) and the divisional bulletin boards.

Some examples of why employees received the honor were for:

- Sharing knowledge
- Productivity/cost savings/quality
- Consistent, exceptional service
- Exceptional work habits
- Follow-up
- Strives for excellence–tries the hardest
- Courteous/community service/problem solving
- Teambuilder

- Most improved attitude

We were uncertain as to how well accepted the Golden Attitude program would be since DFS already had an "Employee of the Year" program in place for three years. This program was developed and managed by employees with no management involvement. Each year, six employees were honored by their peers with $250 and two days annual leave awards, plus significant publicity. In comparison, the Golden Attitude program had minimal cash involved and was developed and was managed by management with some employee involvement (anyone could nominate an employee within their division).

Training in the department was continuous and added more opportunities in other areas, subjects that were closely tied to building and maintaining a positive attitude. Team building, goal setting, breaking down paradigms and improving interpersonal skills seminars were offered. More than 60 employees attended the Zig Ziglar, in-person, four-hour success seminars where they had the opportunity to meet and be photographed with Zig. All employees also received specially designed T-shirts each year that said "DFS....Where Attitude Is the Difference," "110%," and "Quality Is an Attitude" for their enthusiastic acceptance of the program. They were encouraged to wear them to work, which they did with pride.

DFS became licensed to offer its employees the entire *See You at the Top* training series and by the end of December 1993, more than 70 employees were alumni of this 24-hour training program which basically focused on *attitude*. It was the cornerstone of DFS's quality program. By June 1994, 125 of DFS's employees completed this intensive "peoples skills" program and at the time of writing this book, more than 400 county employees completed the program.

One important aspect of the program was that employees volunteered an hour per week of their personal time and Montgomery County matched it by approving an hour of administrative leave for the program.

Phase 4

In setting goals, you can only go as far as you can see, and then go from there. DFS had earned a good image and a good reputation for providing quality customer service. They also had an excellence program in place, based on Tom Peters' philosophy. DFS management decided that the "increments to excellence" program, where managers started each weekly staff meeting with a quality accomplishment by each division, was very important and could be further improved and expanded to employees.

In July 1993 we implemented our "quality is an attitude" program which focused on employee empowerment and our vision of "100% employee involvement." The criteria included:

- Employee submitted a quality increment of excellence to his/her manager.
- Manager determined if the increment would be an improvement, savings or revenue producer and presented it at weekly staff meetings as a quality increment.
- If the idea was an improvement, a silver token was presented to the employee.
- When a savings or revenue was achieved, a gold token was presented to the employee.
- After the employee was rewarded *five* tokens, he/she was presented with a quality pin. If all five tokens were *gold*, a $100 gift certificate was awarded.
- For every *five additional silver or gold* tokens, $100 gift certificates were also awarded.
- In early June 1994, a celebration occurred where all quality pin recipients, managers, and the quality leadership team gathered together and presented cash awards to those deserving employees who were awarded the most number of tokens. Most of DFS' $5,000 total monetary awards' allocation from a non-departmental account was utilized for this program. This was in addition to nearly $15,000 worth of gift certificates.

By the end of fiscal year 1994 (June 30, 1993) 250 employees produced 1142 approved quality increments, representing a savings/new revenue of more than $2,600,000, a ROI of more than 125:1. Not bad, considering the total investment in the program was $20,000.

In fiscal year 1995 the department set a new motto, "10% More Than '94." Employees who submitted six or more quality increments would be recognized with a 110% pin and cash awards, totaling more than $30,000, were given out through the year. *Eighty-eight percent* of all employees submitted an approved increment and by year end, nearly 1,200 additional quality increments were accepted, adding more than $2,000,000 in additional savings/new revenue.

Montgomery County, Maryland officials decided to invest in total quality management (TQM) throughout its 41 agencies/departments in January 1992. In justifying the TQM program for the entire county (pop. 827,000), DFS was singled out for its innovative programs and for the results it achieved for implementing its in-house excellence and attitude programs. That recognition surely propelled our status in the organization and significantly affected our image.

In the first two years, DFS was able to raise revenues by $1.5M/year and use its savings to pay for $1.3M/year in unbudgeted deferred maintenance, as well as all of its training. The total training budget was approximately $30,000, an insignificant amount for a department with 250 total employees. Other county departments followed DFS' lead and many other good things happened since the program began. In early 1993, DFS' Attitude Program was nominated for two national "Innovations in Government" competitions. Since then, DFS has been awarded four national awards. Also, DFS has been featured in Montgomery County's *Total Quality Management* newsletter for exemplary customer service and became a feature story in the May/June 1993 issue of *Top Performance* magazine.

More than 1400 county employees have attended the 2-1/2 hour attitude program initiated by DFS in August 1991 and more than 6,000 private and public sector employees outside of Montgomery

County have also attended this program. Three other county agencies have been licensed to offer the Ziglar training program and approximately 400 county employees completed Ziglar's *See You at the Top* and *Strategies for Success* programs. *Strategies for Success* replaced *See You at the Top* training programs and is a six-week, two-hours per week program, still popular and offered county-wide as a fundamental training program in people skills and values. Was this program an effective way to gain recognition: I think so. For more, read *Looking for the Gold* and *Creative Leadership: Mining the Gold in Your Workforce.*

SUMMARY

Facilities management will be a challenging profession in the twenty-first century, requiring a new level of facilities manager who will emerge out of the backroom and take on additional responsibilities other than pure facilities under his/her wings. All sorts of exciting opportunities await the facilities professional who is a continual learner and develops leadership skills similar to those contained in this book. I sincerely hope that you enjoy it and the information in my book helps you achieve your goals of becoming the best "you" can be. You can accomplish your dreams by *looking for the gold in others. When you do, you'll always find the gold in you.*

13

A CASE STUDY OF A
SUCCESSFUL FM
DEPARTMENT

The Montgomery County government employs more than 8,000 workers to support a population of more than 800,000 residents, and occupies 4 million square feet of space distributed among hundreds of county government facilities. The bulk of the responsibility for administration of these facilities rests with the Montgomery County Department of Facilities and Services (DFS). The department's structure is modeled after traditional functional lines, with four primary functional areas organized as divisions of the department. The divisions include:

The Real Estate Management Division. Twelve employees, involved in the administration of the county's leasing, property management, land acquisition and disposition programs.

The Capital Projects Management Division. Thirty-one employees, involved in the administration of the design and construction processes for new county facilities.

The Facilities Operation and Maintenance Division. Eighty-one employees, charged with ongoing facility maintenance for county buildings.

The General Services Division. Ninety-six employees, providing building services, mail and printing, security and food services.

The Office of the Director. Provides leadership, coordination and staff support to the divisions.

This case study is based on the experiences of DFS in 1991-1994, during development and implementation of its total quality management program. The process-conscious nature of government can make it difficult to breed excitement and build true commitment to excellence. Often, the best of intentions in government are negated by an absence of focus on the target. During these three years, DFS has endeavored to overcome these systemic obstacles by embarking on a methodical campaign to win employee commitment to quality. The effort has, indeed, sparked a revolution in our organizational culture, yielding surprising results in the areas of productivity, quality management and superior public service. These experiences have been chronicled in the book entitled *Looking for the Gold*, authored by A.S. Migs Damiani, who served as Director of DFS during much of this time. We hope that the following summary of our experiences and accomplishments will be as impressive to other similar departments as they have been rewarding and exciting for us at DFS.

THE LEADERSHIP FACTOR

The freshest and richest of ingredients will languish and wilt unattended on a kitchen countertop, until and unless a skillful chef can combine them into a successful recipe. The senior management team at DFS were the skillful chefs who, in the spring of 1991, resolved to get cooking. The economic slump that affected much of the country in the early 1990s served as the catalyst for change.

Facing reduced funding and increased demand for services, the DFS managers drafted a blueprint for increased productivity along multiple parallel tracks.

Clarity of Purpose

A strong identity and sense of purpose are the hallmarks of successful organizations. To be truly effective, a team must identify and capitalize on its strengths, acknowledge and address its weaknesses, and recognize opportunities and threats existing in its operational environment. At DFS, the management team organized a series of employee "excellence workshops" designed to bring these factors into focus, and enlist the employees in the development of an action plan. First on the agenda was the study, by all employees, of the organization's past and current performance, discussions of alternative "futures," and identification of areas where the organization excels and areas that need development. The direction of these discussions, although moderated by the management team, were left entirely up to the participating DFS employees, under the assertion that any resulting product would not wholly belong to (and therefore be wholly embraced by) the employees, unless it was the direct, undiluted product of their discussions.

A Strong Direction

An early objective of these employee forums was the development of a clear mission statement for the organization. Many themes were discussed, chief among them the ideas of innovation, challenge, attitude, excellence, customer service and individual dedication. The sincerity and eagerness of the employees were in evidence in the difficulty they experienced in the expression of a mission statement that was brief and concise. Had all of the employees' ideas been combined, the department's mission statement would have been several paragraphs. Ultimately, the mission was declared to involve two opportunities: the chance to address the challenges posed by the economic recession, and the organization's unique position to develop truly innovative ways to address these challenges. The department's mission became "Meeting Today's Challenges with Innovative Solutions." The mission statement, lofty as it sounds, did not contribute any more to the organization's sense of direction than did the vigorous discussions which led to its adoption. In the self-analysis and dialogue about the organization, the employees themselves began the process of defining the direction toward which the common efforts would be deployed.

Development of a Culture

The DFS managers seized on the enthusiasm generated by the employee forums, to reinforce and supplement the themes discussed by the employees, and to fashion therewith the makings of a culture founded on quality and customer service. The department director led a series of workshops, attended by all employees in groups of 50. These workshops were formatted as open discussions with the director, on topics including customer service, quality, team building and attitude. Success stories, accomplishments, and instances of exceptional customer service were shared and discussed by the employees. A "success ethic" began to develop, whereby failure (or lack of effort) was simply not accepted by the group. Achievement as the norm was the overriding goals. Employees' enthusiasm for this new direction was fueled by other departments, which began to acknowledge the growing DFS record of accomplishments, and began to emulate the methods and practices of DFS within their own units. Symbols began to make their way into the department's life. Golden attitude lapel pins were distributed to employees on the nomination of their peers. Weekly nominations would be accepted by the division chiefs from employees wishing to recognize co-workers who contributed to the department's mission and goals. Celebrations would then be held once a month, where the selected employees would receive their attitude lapel pin, coffee mugs, balloons, certificates and other mementos, and generally be recognized by their co-workers for their contributions to the team. Of little intrinsic value, these items were priceless in terms of their symbolism and value to the recipients. Each of these steps added a layer to the growing sense of cohesion and belonging within DFS, and to the developing culture centered around quality and productivity.

Communication

Recognizing that rich, frequent communication nourishes creativity and innovation, the senior managers at DFS established a multifaceted communication network to ensure constant vertical and horizontal exchange. Among the components of this network are:

- Frequent "review and analysis" meetings, wherein each of the divisions presents and discusses progress on each of its programs and projects. The presentations are not made by division management, but rather by the actual project or program leaders. These are open meetings, to which all staff is invited. All divisions are generally represented, leading to exchange, coordination, adjustments, and constant refinement. Participation is welcomed and encouraged. Discussion is lively and productive.
- Regular weekly staff meetings between division managers and the director's office. At these meetings, weekly progress and productivity are discussed among senior managers in the department.
- Monthly "reading file" where all outgoing correspondence from the department is placed. This file is circulated to all divisions, so that each may be familiar with and follow the progress of the other's projects and programs.
- Regular "brown bag lunch" sessions. All employees are invited to bring their lunch and listen to presentations by other employees on interesting aspects of their work. These sessions are designed to expose operational teams to the work of other teams, and to elicit new ideas and innovative approaches from participants.

- Encouragement of a collegial, open atmosphere, conducive to communication. Much of the business of the department is conducted in the hallways. This "management by walking around" is practiced by all managers, beginning with the department director.

- Frequent communication by senior management of the values, beliefs and culture of DFS to other units of county government and to organizations in the private sector. As spokesman for the department, the DFS director led seminars and attitude sessions with teams of employees from other County departments, groups of local high school students, the staff from a nearby hospital, large groups from the Association for Facilities Engineering and others outside of DFS. The director also made presentations to local governments from other states, including Orange County, Florida, and local private sector employers in the Washington area. Had he not been prevented by common sense and a reasonable concern for safety, the director would have sung the praises of DFS with a bullhorn from the rooftop of our building.

Recognition

If nothing else, DFS celebrates! Public celebrations of the things that contribute to the strengthening of culture, linked to accomplishment of strategic objectives, were held religiously. No opportunity was wasted to encourage, applaud, cheer and honor achievement. Recognition by one's peers was held in the highest regard, and the most significant celebrations were therefore reserved for programs where the employees themselves selected the honorees. Notable among the many programs devised to commend success were:

- The "Golden Attitude" program mentioned above, instituted in 1992, whereby employees were honored by nomination of their peers for excellence in the areas of productivity, sharing of knowledge, customer service, teamwork, follow-up and a number of other criteria;

- The "Employee of the Year" celebration, which was a large gathering of all department employees, to select six employees that exemplify the DFS commitment to quality and superior public service. Again, this program relied on nominations from co-workers. The final selections were also made by committees comprised of employees. Amid a sea of balloons and music, the six annual winners were toasted in an auditorium by the entire staff.

- The "Quality Increment Program," instituted in 1993, which rewarded employees with recognition, gift certificates, and annual leave periodically throughout the year, culminating in a large annual celebration of the largest contributors. This was a particularly successful program, where employees were encouraged to submit new ideas, new ways to do things, resulting in savings, new revenues or improvements in the quality of service. During fiscal year 1994, this program yielded more than 1,100 substantial operational improvements, all of which were implemented by the organization, resulting in cost savings and new revenues of more than $2.6 million. More about this in the Results section.

- The "C.A.O. Citation" which was awarded annually by management to several employees who made extraordinary contributions toward the organization's objectives.

These programs were supplemented by dozens of other informal, impromptu celebrations, certificates and awards handed out to employees for specific instances of exemplary service to the customer, or accomplishments in productivity and efficiency. The overriding goal was to ensure that achievement was consistently recognized.

Strategic Planning

Tactical success can only be sustained for a short period of time, in the absence of a strategic plan. The Quality Council, composed of DFS senior management, laid out a leadership agenda, spanning a period of five years, and outlining the longer term objectives of the organization, as well as the proposed means of reaching those objectives. Operational objectives relating to the accomplishment or advancement of specific projects and programs were an important part of this plan. However, areas relating to the reinforcement and enhancement of culture, the improvement of processes, and the development of teams and individuals were just as prominent. The leadership agenda was not a "top-down" plan. It flowed directly from the annual work programs of each employee, coordinated up through project and section plans, forming part of each divisional leadership agenda, ultimately coordinated into the integrated department leadership agenda. In this way, each and every individual employee effort towards attainment of individual goals contributed to the advancement of short and long term organizational objectives. Dynamic and constantly changing, the leadership agenda features specific goals in the following target areas:

- Employee training
- Knowledge of the customer
- Boundary spanning
- Process improvement
- Automation
- Information
- Technical training
- Organizational structure
- New revenues
- Time management
- Efficiency and productivity
- Service "marketing"
- Cost savings

The agenda is constantly under review and reassessment, to refine direction, adjust targets and redirect effort as warranted to move toward goals. It is a flexible plan that gives purpose and defines the objectives, while allowing for tactical maneuvers needed to adapt to changing circumstances.

PEOPLE AS THE CRITICAL RESOURCE

As a service organization, the single most important resource available to us at DFS is our people. Unlike a manufacturing business, we cannot rely on the strength of our product for success. At DFS, our people *are* our product. Accordingly, a great deal of care and attention are devoted to the development, training, recruitment and improvement of this most critical resource.

Empowerment

The pride of ownership is the most compelling motivator. At DFS, the people own the "company." Each employee has come to regard his or her work program as his or her own small business. As "business owners," we have both the authority and responsibility to conduct our business in a way that is efficient, effective and, above all, pleasing to the customer. To tap into the strength that comes from diversity, challenging projects are often tackled by autonomous "QATs" or quality action teams. These are intra-divisional groups of people with different technical and professional backgrounds, who can each make a distinct yet cumulatively powerful contribution to resolving a problem or seizing and opportunity. These quality action teams act largely independent of management. Their target is the leadership agenda. Items from the agenda are selected by teams, who will work on the item during regular team meetings, and who report to management on progress from time to time. Members may serve in several quality action teams, each pursuing a different goal, and bringing to each team the experiences gained on the work of other teams. In addition to service on quality action teams, employees also pursue their individual work programs along the functional areas of each division. In this way, the people carry on a rich and productive matrix-like buzz of activity, with frequent communication and coordination, constant learning, sharing of knowledge and information, cross-training and expansion of professional boundaries. The high level of skill and judgment of the DFS employees make it possible for much of this work to be carried on with minimal supervision from management. Employees are encouraged to take charge of their work, and take on responsibility for accomplishment of the objectives, with full authority to "do the right thing."

Training and Personal Development

The degree of autonomy and responsibility granted to the DFS employees is possible only because of the investment made by the organization in training. The training opportunities made available were carefully balanced to support and promote the organization's strategic plan. They included technical training, development of analytical and thinking skills, cultural and organizational values re-inforcement, attitude and customer service, total quality, cross-divisional training and many others. The underlying theme in the DFS approach to training was an unequivocal commitment to con-tinuous learning. Although the list of specific courses, programs and seminars is too extensive to list here, a few notable programs deserve some space:

The department instituted a comprehensive, seven-week train-ing program in the principles and practices of total quality manage-ment, with the objective of reaching each and every employee in DFS. Working with the Maryland Center for Quality and Produc-tivity, a total quality management training guide was developed for the department, addressing questions such as quality awareness; the forces for change in the public section; paradigm shifts; principles for good government; personal commitment to excellence; problem resolution and facilitation techniques; analytical tools; meeting skills and many other areas. This guide was used as a basis for total quality management discussions with all employees over the course of several sessions. Initial sessions with the quality leadership team were facilitated by the department's Deputy Director. The quality leadership team was comprised of 50 "role model" employees and division chiefs, who held their own regular discussions over the course of the following several months with all remaining employees, using the same materials.

A twelve-week course of instruction in goal setting, communication, and personal development based on Zig Ziglar's "See You at the Top Lifetime Results" program was offered to employees in 1992. The deputy director received specialized training to lead these seminars from the Zig Ziglar Corporation. The series of seminars were so popular, many employees attended the sessions outside of normal work hours, on their own time! "Graduation" from the program was an excuse for yet another celebration, with employees' supervisors, and often friends and family in attendance.

Brown bag luncheon sessions are held regularly in the department's main conference room, where employees make presentations to other employees about their programs, successes and exciting new initiatives that are under development. These cross-training opportunities are valued by employees, who learn about the work of other teams in the department, and often contribute to lively discussions on potential process improvements.

Excellence seminars are held for all employees semi-annually by the department director, to celebrate accomplishments, review tactical and strategic plans, reinforce organizational values and discuss progress toward goals.

These are but a few of the opportunities available to DFS employees. Other seminars and programs regularly offered address teamwork, interpersonal communications, cultural awareness and sensitivity, Toastmasters Club, computer skills, writing skills and many others.

Individual Contributions

The department's agenda truly runs on and is fueled by many individual contributions. They are called "quality increments" in DFS, under the assertion that excellence is not reached in one dramatic leap, but rather in the cumulative, incremental contributions of many people, working toward the same goal. This idea moved from theory to practice in the spring of 1993, with the official inauguration of the quality increment program. Although individual employee contributions to productivity and efficiency had been encouraged and celebrated at DFS for several years, the quality increment program institutionalized the practice, fused it into the organizational culture, and established a tighter link between individual contributions and reward and recognition programs.

Briefly stated, the quality increment program was designed to acknowledge concrete individual and team contributions to organizational goals in cost savings, generation of new revenue, process improvements and customer service. Employee contributions were submitted to and evaluated by senior management. Employees reaching pre-established goals were rewarded with gift certificates, annual leave, and recognition of their peers. Annual goals were set to benchmark against the best organizations in the private sector who had instituted similar employee contributions programs. The DFS goal was set at 1,000 quality increments for fiscal year 1994, which represented an average of more than four quality increments per employee. Divisions were also encouraged to compete against one another in terms of their average performance, with end-of-year recognition for the best divisional achievement.

The response was enthusiastic, and exceeded the expectations of the DFS managers in every respect. In a department with 246 employees, 205 participated in the program, representing a very substantial 83% participation rate. The following table summarizes overall participation statistics and results.

Measurement	Results
FY 94 Increment Goal	1,000
FY 94 Increments Achieved	1,142
Exceeded Goal By	14.2%
Number of Increments Submitted	1,511
Number of Increments Approved	1,142
Approved as % of Submitted	76%
New Revenue Generated	$608,809
Cost Savings Realized	$2,047,877
Total Revenue/Savings	$2,656,686

The financial gain to the organization, although very substantial, was overshadowed by the gains in quality, productivity and customer service. Although more difficult to quantify than savings and revenue, the new ideas and vast improvements in the way things are done will bring a greater yield to the organization in the long run. A complete listing of the many contributions would be impossible within the format of this submission, but a more detailed summary of the results will be included in the "Results" section. The most significant outcome of this program was a confirmation of the power of individuals who, when properly motivated and channeled, will surprise even the most optimistic manager.

Workforce Readiness

A merging of organizational and individual goals can only be accomplished if both the organization and individual respect each other's needs and work together to fulfill them. The organization requested contributions and commitments from the employees to further productivity and efficiency. In turn, the organization makes contributions to employees to simplify and enhance their lives and promote their health and well being. In addition to the County-wide "Work-Life" program, which provides alternative work schedules, flex time, telecommuting, priority placement in local day care centers, professional sabbaticals, and many other opportunities,

DFS opened several avenues on its own, to improve the quality of life for its employees. Some examples:

- Some of the DFS managers volunteered to conduct literacy sessions for employees who needed assistance in developing their reading and writing skills.
- DFS converted an unused area in a nearby county building into a shower, work-out and locker room facility for the convenience of employees wishing to jog or exercise during the day.
- A Wellness Committee, composed of employees, was set up to develop and implement ways to improve employee health, including lunch time walks, exercise programs, weight control, smoking cessation courses, video presentations and many others.
- Family participation in the work life of employees is encouraged. Many opportunities are made available to employees to bring their families to socialize and become a part of the organizational setting, including the annual picnic, departmental celebrations, graduation from employee training programs, etc.
- A full kitchen was installed for employees, so that food preparation and storage is available for those who choose. This provides a more economical and healthful way for employees to prepare lunch, and is a good alternative to fast food.

Employee Satisfaction

The DFS employees feel that they "own" their workplace. They want to come to work, and they enjoy the daily give and take within the team. There have been only three employee grievances filed since 1991. As an annualized percentage, and based on the department's personnel complement, this represents a statistically negligible one-third of one percent of the workforce.

Attendance and absenteeism rates are equally impressive. In fiscal year 1993, the department instituted a "perfect attendance" program, intended to recognize employees who use less than eight hours sick leave during the fiscal year. The following graph shows the employees' response to this program since its inception:

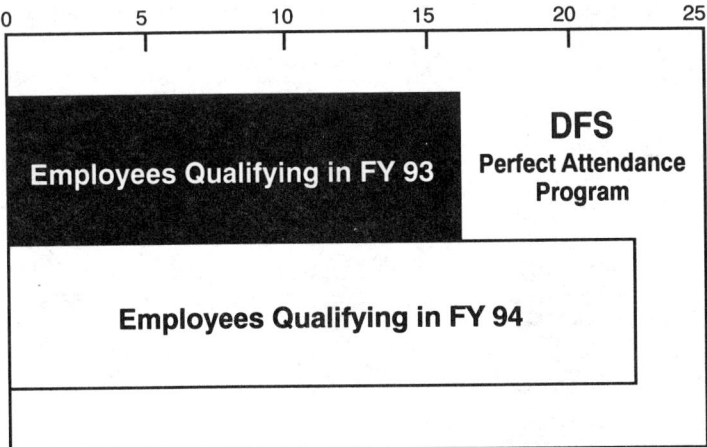

In fiscal year 1994, nearly 10% of the employees workforce qualified in recognition under the perfect attendance program. From 1993 to 1994, the number of employees qualifying for this honor increased by 44%.

Employee turnover is also minimal, indicating strong satisfaction with the department's policies, the organizational environment and the management team. In calendar years 1991 and 1992, annual employee turnover was a very low 2.5% of the workforce. This rate competes with the very best organizations in the public and private sectors. In 1993, already low rates decreased further, by more than 50%, to an annual rate of only 1.2%. Annualized data so far for 1994 shows that the 1.2% turnover rate will be maintained in 1994.

RESULTS—PRODUCTIVITY AND QUALITY

The organization's efforts in motivation, training, planning, and empowerment have yielded significant results in the areas of effectiveness, efficiency and improved productivity. The summary data is impressive, but it is the individual accomplishments, like bricks in a building, that truly tell the story. As the following graph shows, the department's actual level of expense has fallen in the last three years, while its responsibilities, in terms of building space maintained, have increased.

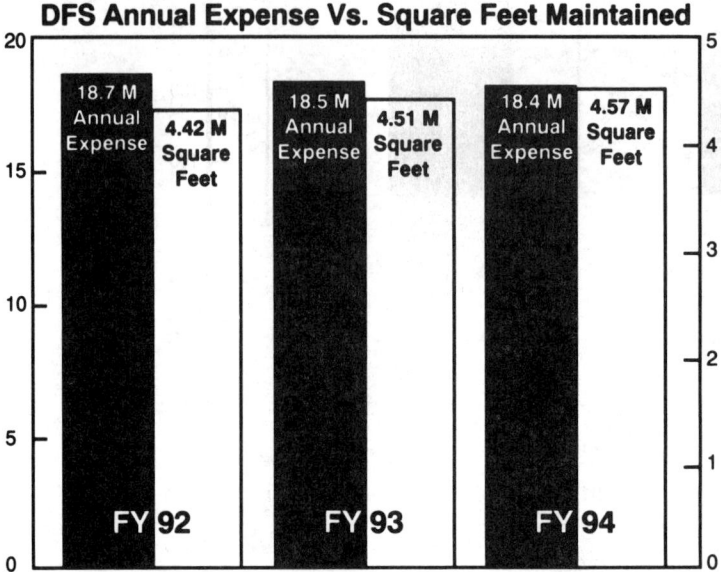

Along with responsibility, the quality of service has also increased. This has been possible through many contributions which are modest individually, but formidable in the aggregate. In this section we attempt, within the limited available space, to describe some of the representative achievements made by employees of DFS, both at the departmental as well as the individual level.

In the Real Estate Management Area

Through hard-nose renegotiation of contracts, seizing opportunities in the market and other efficiency measures, the real estate management division has reduced the rental expense budget by 20% since fiscal year 1992. In the last two fiscal years, the downward trend in the annual rental expense budget has continued, despite an increase in the total number of square feet leased.

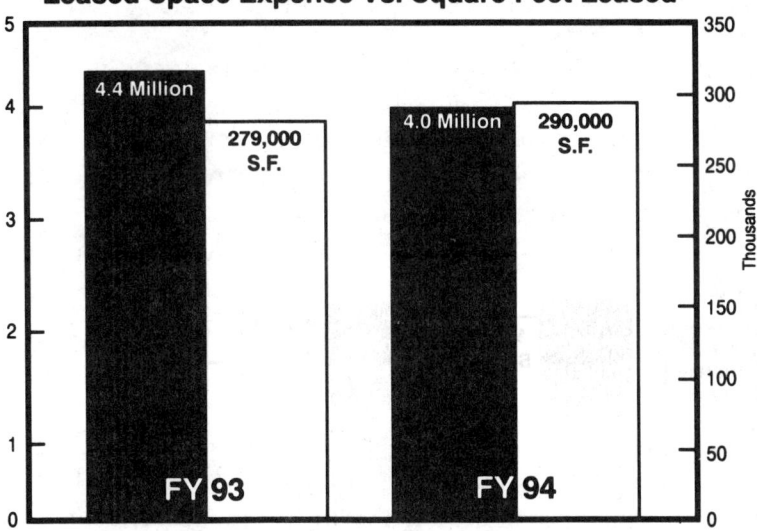

Leased Space Expense Vs. Square Feet Leased

FY 93: 4.4 Million — 279,000 S.F.
FY 94: 4.0 Million — 290,000 S.F.

On an individual level, the real estate management employees have made substantial contributions to productivity. Although numbering in the hundreds, some of the representative ideas and process improvements implemented include:

- Saving the county demolition and removal costs for an old log smokehouse located on county property by offering it to a local farmer interested in historic preservation. The structure was disassembled and reassembled nearby on private property at no cost to the county.
- Employees in the moving section designed a new equipment and book cart to use for moves of offices and equipment, resulting in better service, increased productivity and savings of $2,500 per year in rental costs. The employees of the maintenance division built the carts.
- Negotiated lease of small unused county parcels in the urban sections of the county to local restaurants for evening parking, putting the properties to productive use and generating revenues for the county.
- Established a cross-reference system to make it easier for tenants of the county's closed schools to identify suitable sub-tenants to help use vacant space and defray the tenant's facility expenses.

In the Maintenance Area

Employees of the maintenance division submitted 286 new ideas, which were implemented by the department, resulting in dramatic efficiency increases and improved service to the customer, while reducing costs. Reusing old parts, making maximum use of in-house capabilities and constantly scanning for service improvements yielded significant benefits to the organization. Representative contributions include:

- Using a discarded pyrotronics fire alarm control panel, the maintenance employees built a working fire alarm model, to train electric shop personnel on the installation and troubleshooting of solid state fire alarm systems.
- Designed, built and installed devices on the rooftops of plumbing section vehicles that allow for water piping to be carried atop the vehicles, making more room available for tools, equipment and personnel inside.
- Extended the life and improved the performance of cooling tower floats by 10 to 15 years, by injecting them with dry foam.
- Designed and modified the decks at one of the county's aquatic centers to allow for in-house cleaning of the drains without the need to hire specialized contractors.

In the General Services Area

In the department's largest division, 80% of the ideas submitted by employees were implemented, resulting in 357 individual increments to improve operations and productivity. Representative contributions include:

- The print shop devised a method to mix standard printing inks for special colors in-house, rather than to incur the time and expense involved in ordering special color inks.

- Initiated a program at the county's detention center to allow inmates who enjoy and are knowledgeable about landscaping to maintain landscaped areas inside the detention center's recreation yard.
- To increase customer participation in the less expensive bulk mailing, the mail room instituted a "sale" whereby customer's budgets would only be charged 1 cent for each item of bulk mail submitted. Response was enthusiastic. Savings are expected to be significant this year.
- Recycled cardboard cores that are provided with rolls of engineering paper as containers to be used for mailing plans and specifications.
- The need for cleaning of the public restrooms in the central county office buildings increased in the winter due to use by homeless people. The general services division organized the homeless, who volunteered to clean the restrooms themselves, with the county providing cleaning supplies.

In the Capital Projects Management Area

The employees responsible for design, engineering and construction of county buildings made very significant strides toward more efficient building design and improvements to the capital program process. Ninety-seven percent of the employees in this division participated in fiscal year 1994, submitting 134 new ideas, among them:

- Successful marketing of their services, persuading another county agency to assign projects totaling $6 million to be carried out by the capital projects management division.
- Converted the EMS system to a micro-computer based configuration, improving service and saving annual maintenance contract costs of $60,000.
- Developed energy efficiency design guidelines for use in the design of county buildings, which have found a very receptive

audience in the private sector, and with other local government jurisdictions. Many copies of the guidelines have been sold, resulting in a new revenue source for the county, with sales to date in the thousands.

- Garnered the 1993 PTI Technology Achievement Award for "Quality Management Brings New Value to Government Construction."
- Won 1993 AIPE "FAME" Award for their entry, entitled "Building Energy Design Program."
- Implemented installation of LED emergency exit signs, countywide, at a cost of $98,000—and then arranged for a rebate for the work from PEPCO in the amount of $95,000.

In all, more than 1,100 incremental improvements were implemented in fiscal year 1994, yielding more than $2 million in direct cost savings to the department, and more than $600,000 in new revenues collected as a result of the individual efforts of 246 employees. The combined savings and revenue results for fiscal year 1994 represents an average contribution of more than $10,000 per employee, and constitute 15% of the department's budget. In fiscal year 1995 a new goal was set, "to achieve ten percent more than '94" in terms of productivity and quality increases.

RESULTS—CUSTOMER ORIENTATION

Constant communication with the customer is of paramount importance. Success is more a function of customer perception than it is a product of numbers and statistics. At DFS, we're not doing a good job until the customer says we're doing a good job. To that end, many avenues have been developed to maintain and enhance relationships with customers that will allow us to measure progress according to the one all important yardstick of success—customer satisfaction.

Customer Forums

All divisions in DFS conduct periodic customer "quality forums." where representatives of each customer group are invited to discuss DFS performance along functional lines. Progress on current projects is discussed, as well as potential process improvements, ways to enhance communication, address deficient areas and recognize accomplishments of note. At these forums, customers are encouraged to challenge the way we operate and to make suggestions for improving service. Invariably, the forums provide useful insights to DFS as to customer expectations, perceptions of the quality of our service, and concrete ideas that can be put to productive use.

Customer Surveys

The relationship with the customer is an ongoing concern. To cultivate this relationship, we must have continually updated information. Surveys are therefore used with frequency by the DFS divisions, to ask for customer feedback on topics as varied as the quality of the cafeteria products and services, the efficiency of our in-house mail service, satisfaction with copy machine quality, maintenance team response and efficiency, the effectiveness of our capital projects development process, and many others. Some of the divisions in DFS have even established customer survey databases, where the results of customer surveys are stored by category, to allow for more detailed examination of responses, in order to identify patterns and areas of concern, and ultimately refine service.

Customer Education

As a service department, we are eager to show and make our capabilities available to the customer. As new programs and services develop, DFS insures that their availability is known by constant communication with, and education of, the customers. The DFS divisions began publication of manuals in 1990, intended to provide the DFS customers with a handy, yet comprehensive, listing of DFS services available and instruction on how to access these services. These manuals became as essential to the customers as the county phone directory. In 1993, DFS consolidated all departmental information into a full department service manual, which is published and delivered to customers annually, with more frequent updates as changes warrant. This DFS service manual details all products, trades, technical and professional support services and resources available through DFS, and provides the customer with staff assignments, telephone numbers, maps, and all information needed for the customer to avail itself of the full DFS capabilities.

The Little Things

All print jobs completed by the DFS print shop are returned to the customer with a note. The note, in addition to thanking the customer for the work, includes the name of the staff person who completed the job, so that any problems may be addressed immediately by the worker involved. When a county agency first moves into a leased facility, the staff of the real estate management division presents the new tenant with a "welcome folder." The folder is printed with the DFS mission statement, and contains reduced copies of the tenant's floor plans for future reference, important lease information, rules and regulations of note, parking instructions, DFS contacts and telephone stickers with the DFS phone number for quick access to service. The moving crew provides refrigerator magnets to customers, shaped like a moving truck, featuring the phone number of the moving section, so that customers can quickly call to have furniture or equipment rearranged if it becomes necessary. Old parking permits are provided to local day care centers so that they can be used by the children for art and craft projects. These are small, inexpensive vehicles to communicate and reinforce the more significant message that the customer is the single overriding reason that we are in business—and that the customer's satisfaction is our primary target.

Making the Customer a Partner

The customer is not viewed as an external entity, but rather as much a part of the department as the department's employees or managers. Customers are celebrated right along with DFS employees when accomplishments are made or goals are reached. The employees of DFS customers are honored by DFS frequently, with public praise, certificates and tokens of appreciation delivered at ceremonies held at the DFS offices. DFS hosts "open houses" to inform and market its services to customers. Customers are invited to make presentations to DFS employees on the nature of their work and the challenges they face. DFS reciprocates by providing similar sessions to instruct and educate other county agencies as to DFS and its mission. Customers are often invited to sit in on management meetings at DFS, and DFS is often represented at internal customer meetings. The exchanges strength the link and solidify the relationship between the organization and its customers.

The Customer Responds

DFS efforts on behalf of its customers have not gone unnoticed. Recent interviews with DFS customers were held by the countywide total quality management unit, as part of an article published in the county government's TQM quarterly. The best and most effective way to convey our success in the area of customer satisfaction is to use the words of the customers themselves, reprinted from this article, entitled "DFS Customers Are Delighted."

> *"Julie Morris of the County Council staff is also a frequent customer of DFS, and says she has seen a vast improvement in recent years in DFS service. According to Julie, it is as if DFS employees have blossomed. She is particularly impressed with the way they ware constantly thinking of better ways to solve a problem. Julie recalled an incident that occurred during the renovation of the Council Office*

Building. A subcontractor was supposed to install veneer on the rostrum in the seventh floor hearing room, but showed up with materials that did not match the existing wood. The DFS carpenter shop came to the rescue and worked over a holiday to install the right veneer."

"Two other extremely satisfied customers are the regional librarians at the Bethesda and Rockville libraries. Leila Shapiro of the Bethesda Library says their recent rehabilitation work went smoothly because of the DFS staff and, in particular, Roy Howes, the project manager. Leila says Roy was on site every day, had a written plan of action, communicated with her daily about every detail, and had an excellent relationship with the contractor. Brian Auger of the Rockville Library was equally impressed with the work of DFS. They, too, recently had rehabilitation work, and Brian was especially impressed with the responsiveness of two DFS employees, Wayne Nebel and Al Roshdieh, who he says listened to their needs and really worked to satisfy all requests."

"Naomi Sapir, an Administrative Specialist in the Department of Addiction, Victim and Mental Health Services, says she acts as a liaison to DFS for her department, on everything from cleaning services, to maintenance at their 14 facilities, to moving, to capital projects. Naomi says she is more than satisfied with the service she receives from DFS. She says that DFS employees are caring and understanding, extremely responsive, and go out of their way to work with her to find solutions that will meet her needs."

There is no more accurate, nor more effective measure of the degree to which an organization is meeting the needs of its customers than the customer's own expressions of appreciation. In the last few years, DFS has received hundreds of individual letters of commendation, which customers felt compelled to write to thank

DFS employees for exceeding customer expectations. This is the true yardstick by which success can be assessed.

COMMUNITY IMPACT

Ultimately, the accomplishments of DFS inure to the benefit of the community at large. Increased productivity, cost savings and improvements in the quality of service allow economic resources to be released and redeployed to address other areas of concern to the citizens and taxpayers of our county and state. The DFS contributions to the community have not only been economic. The methods, techniques and experiences of DFS with quality management have been made available to many other organizations at the local, state and national level, in the hopes that they may serve to improve the productivity of others. Within the parent organization, DFS has presented workshops on attitude and quality to many other County departments and agencies. To date, more than 1,100 county employees outside of DFS have attended DFS seminars outlining our culture and encouraging emulation. Sessions have been held by DFS on quality and the importance of attitude with groups of Montgomery County junior and senior high school students. DFS has made presentations on its quality programs to groups from four separate counties in Maryland's eastern shore, and to county government representatives from jurisdictions as far away as Orange County, Florida. Workshops based on the DFS experience have been held by the DFS Director at two general sessions of the Maryland Association of Counties. Staff from three Maryland hospitals have participated in DFS empowerment and attitude seminars. In the private and academic sectors, several companies have asked for and received sessions by DFS on the elements of our quality management program, including the Up-John Company, Westwood-Squibb, and the James Madison University. The American Institute of Plant Engineers was so impressed with the DFS program and record of performance that we have been invited to provide sessions at six of their national and regional conferences. To date, more than 1,500 people in organizations outside of DFS have attended the seminars and workshops provided by DFS as part of its outreach efforts.

The DFS interest in the advancement and welfare of its community extends to environmental awareness as well. We are generally recognized within the county government as leaders in the promotion of the county's recycling efforts. DFS has performed waste audits at more than 25 facilities to date, in order to determine recyclabes in the waste stream, and refine our recycling efforts. DFS has instituted and managed many programs to examine and implement the reuse of resources, including the recycling of phone books and the use of recycled asphalt at county facilities.

We have pursued and received grants from the Urban Consortium energy task force to develop management plans to convert cooling systems to eliminate ozone-depleting refrigerants. A report on this issue was presented by DFS at the 1992 International CFC and Halon Alternative Conference. We have received a grant from the Maryland Energy Administration, to establish an energy design center. The purpose of the center is to export the DFS award-winning energy conservation program to state agencies. We have received more than $600,000 in utility rebates for energy conservation projects. Our efforts in these areas continue.

The above was extracted from a US Senate Productivity Award and Maryland Excellence Award1994/1995 competition.

ORDER ADDITIONAL COPIES OF BOOKS BY MIGS DAMIANI! CALL 1-800-488-8040 OR USE THIS HANDY FORM.

3 EASY WAYS TO ORDER!

Mail in an envelope to
100 Newfield
Ave, Edison NJ
08837

Call toll-free
1-800-488-8040

Fax order to
(732)
225-1562

Unless otherwise indicated, shipping/handling charge is $3.00 for first copy and $1.00 for each additional copy. Special offers good for book rate USPS shipments to private individuals in US and Canada only. New Jersey residents add 6% sales tax.

For orders of 10 copies or more, discounted pricing and lower shipping/handling may apply. Call (973) 543-1115 for a special quote.

Name _____

Company (optional) _____

Address 1 _____

Address 2 _____

City _____

State _____ Zip _____ Country _____

Phone ( ) _____

FAX ( ) _____

Email _____

P.O.# _____

☐ Check enclosed (US dollars)

Credit card: ☐ VISA ☐ MasterCard ☐ Am Express

Card No. _____

Exp. Date ___ / ___

Qty	ISBN	Title	List	Special	S/H	Subtotal
	1-891121-03-0	**Moving Up the Org. in Facilities Mgmt** (Damiani)	$24.95	$21.00		
	1-5744-226-0	**Creative Leadership** (Damiani)	$17.95	$15.00		
	1-891121-05-7	**Moving Up Org. & Creat. Leadrshp.** (both books)	$42.90	$33.50	$4.00	
	n/a - order by title	**Looking for the Gold** (Damiani)	$14.95	$7.50		
	1-891121-06-5	**Set of all three books by Damiani**	$57.85	$37.50	$5.00	
						TOTAL

SciTech Publishing • c/o Whitehurst & Clark • 100 Newfield Ave. • Edison, NJ 08837
Please make checks payable to SciTech Publishing, Inc.